UNIX

FOR

DUMMIES

Quick Reference

First Issue

Collector Edition

by Margaret Levine Young and John R. Levine

IDG BOOKS

IDG Books Worldwide, Inc.
An International Data Group Company

San Mateo, California ♦ Indianapolis, Indiana ♦ Boston, Massachusetts

Unix For Dummies Quick Reference

Published by
IDG Books Worldwide, Inc.
An International Data Group Company
155 Bovet Road, Suite 310
San Mateo, CA 94402

Library of Congress Catalog Card No.: 93-78448

ISBN 1-56884-094-2

Printed in the United States of America

10 9 8 7 6 5 4 3 2 1

Distributed in the United States by IDG Books Worldwide, Inc.

Distributed in Canada by Macmillan of Canada, a Division of Canada Publishing Corporation; by Computer and Technical Books in Miami, Florida, for South America and the Caribbean; by Longman Singapore in Singapore, Malaysia, Thailand, and Korea; by Toppan Co. Ltd. in Japan; by Asia Computerworld in Hong Kong; by Woodslane Pty. Ltd. in Australia and New Zealand; and by Transword Publishers Ltd. in the U.K. and Europe.

For information on where to purchase IDG Books outside the U.S., contact Christina Turner at 415-312-0633.

For information on translations, contact Marc Jeffrey Mikulich, Foreign Rights Manager, at IDG Books Worldwide; FAX NUMBER 415-358-1260.

For sales inquiries and special prices for bulk quantities, write to the address above or call IDG Books Worldwide at 415-312-0650.

COMPUTER
BOOK SERIES
FROM IDG

is a trademark of IDG Books Worldwide, Inc.

Acknowledgments

The authors would like to thank Jordan Young, Lydia Spitzer, Meg Young, Steve Emmerich, and the entire gang at Lexington Playcare Center (especially Cate, Rachel, Bridget, Terri, and Chris) for their support in writing this book. We also want to acknowledge Becky Whitney for her fine editing job and Sandy Grieshop for her sharp proofreading eye.

In addition, we have enjoyed and appreciated the feedback we've gotten from readers of *UNIX For Dummies*. If you have comments about this book, be sure to e-mail us at *dummies@iecc.com*.

The publisher would like to give special thanks to Patrick J. McGovern, without whom this book would not have been possible.

Credits

Publisher
David Solomon

Managing Editor
Mary Bednarek

Acquisitions Editor
Janna Custer

Production Manager
Beth Jenkins

Senior Editors
Tracy L. Barr
Sandy Blackthorn
Diane Graves Steele

Production Coordinator
Cindy L. Phipps

Acquisitions Assistant
Megg Bonar

Editorial Assistant
Patricia R. Reynolds

Project Editor
Rebecca Whitney

Technical Reviewer
Sharon Potter-Newsome

Production Staff
Valery Bourke
Sherry Gomoll
Gina Scott

Proofreader
Sandy Grieshop

Indexer
Sherry Massey

Say What You Think!

Listen up, all you readers of IDG's international bestsellers: the one — the only — absolutely world famous ...*For Dummies* books! It's time for you to take advantage of a new, direct pipeline to the authors and editors of IDG Books Worldwide. In between putting the finishing touches on the next round of ...*For Dummies* books, the authors and editors of IDG Books Worldwide like to sit around and mull over what their readers have to say. And we know that you readers always say what you think. So here's your chance. We'd really like your input for future printings and editions of this book — and ideas for future ...*For Dummies* titles as well. Tell us what you liked (and didn't like) about this book. How about the chapters you found most useful — or most funny? And since we know you're not a bit shy, what about the chapters you think can be improved? Just to show you how much we appreciate your input, we'll add you to our Dummies Database/Fan Club and keep you up to date on the latest ...*For Dummies* books, news, cartoons, calendars, and more! Please send your name, address, and phone number, as well as your comments, questions, and suggestions, to our very own ...*For Dummies* coordinator at the following address:

...For Dummies Coordinator
IDG Books Worldwide
3250 North Post Road, Suite 140
Indianapolis, IN 46226

(Yes, Virginia, there really is a ...*For Dummies* coordinator. We are not making this up.)

Please mention the name of this book in your comments.

Thanks for your input!

About the Author

John Levine and Margaret Levine Young were members of a computer club in high school (this was before high school students, or even high schools, *had* computers.) They came in contact with Theodor H. Nelson, the author of *Computer Lib* and the inventor of hypertext, who fostered the idea that computers should not be taken seriously. He showed them that everyone can understand and use computers.

John wrote his first program in 1967 on an IBM 1130 (a computer roughly as powerful as your typical modern digital wristwatch — only more difficult to use). His first exposure to UNIX was while hanging out with friends in Princeton in 1974; he became an official UNIX system administrator at Yale in 1975. John began working part-time for Interactive Systems, the first commercial UNIX company, in 1977 and has been in and out of the UNIX biz ever since. He used to spend most of his time writing software, but now he mostly writes books because it's more fun. He also teaches some computer courses and publishes and edits an incredibly technoid magazine called *The Journal of C Language Translation.* He has a B.A. and a Ph.D. in computer science from Yale University.

Margy has been using small computers since the 1970s. She graduated from UNIX on a PDP/11 to Apple DOS on an Apple II to MS-DOS and UNIX on a variety of machines. She has done all kinds of jobs that involve explaining to people that computers aren't as mysterious as they might think, including managing the use of PCs at Columbia Pictures, teaching scientists and engineers what computers are good for, and writing computer manuals. She has been president of NYPC, the New York PC Users' Group.

Margy has written several computer books, including *Understanding Javelin PLUS* (John also wrote part of it) and *The Complete Guide to PC-File.* She has a degree in computer science from Yale University.

About IDG Books Worldwide

Welcome to the world of IDG Books Worldwide.

IDG Books Worldwide, Inc., is a division of International Data Group, the world's largest publisher of computer-related information and the leading global provider of information services on information technology. IDG publishes over 194 computer publications in 62 countries. Forty million people read one or more IDG publications each month.

If you use personal computers, IDG Books is committed to publishing quality books that meet your needs. We rely on our extensive network of publications, including such leading periodicals as *Macworld*, *InfoWorld*, *PC World*, *Publish*, *Computerworld*, *Network World*, and *SunWorld*, to help us make informed and timely decisions in creating useful computer books that meet your needs.

Every IDG book strives to bring extra value and skill-building instruction to the reader. Our books are written by experts, with the backing of IDG periodicals, and with careful thought devoted to issues such as audience, interior design, use of icons, and illustrations. Our editorial staff is a careful mix of high-tech journalists and experienced book people. Our close contact with the makers of computer products helps ensure accuracy and thorough coverage. Our heavy use of personal computers at every step in production means we can deliver books in the most timely manner.

We are delivering books of high quality at competitive prices on topics customers want. At IDG, we believe in quality, and we have been delivering quality for over 25 years. You'll find no better book on a subject than an IDG book.

John Kilcullen
President and C.E.O.
IDG Books Worldwide, Inc.

IDG Books Worldwide, Inc. is a division of International Data Group. The officers are Patrick J. McGovern, Founder and Board Chairman; Walter Boyd, President. International Data Group's publications include: **ARGENTINA's** Computerworld Argentina, InfoWorld Argentina; **ASIA's** Computerworld Hong Kong, PC World Hong Kong, Computerworld Southeast Asia, PC World Singapore, Computerworld Malaysia, PC World Malaysia; **AUSTRALIA's** Computerworld Australia, Australian PC World, Australian Macworld, Network World, Reseller, IDG Sources; **AUSTRIA's** Computerwelt Oesterreich, PC Test; **BRAZIL's** Computerworld, Mundo IBM, Mundo Unix, PC World, Publish; **BULGARIA's** Computerworld Bulgaria, Ediworld, PC & Mac World Bulgaria; **CANADA's** Direct Access, Graduate Computerworld, InfoCanada, Network World Canada; **CHILE's** Computerworld, Informatica; **COLOMBIA's** Computerworld Colombia; **CZECH REPUBLIC's** Computerworld, Elektronika, PC World; **DENMARK's** CAD/CAM WORLD, Communications World, Computerworld Danmark, LOTUS World, Macintosh Produktkatalog, Macworld Danmark, PC World Danmark, PC World Produktguide, Windows World; **EQUADOR's** PC World; **EGYPT's** Computerworld (CW) Middle East, PC World Middle East; **FINLAND's** MikroPC, Tietoviikko, Tietoverkko; **FRANCE's** Distributique, GOLDEN MAC, InfoPC, Languages & Systems, Le Guide du Monde Informatique, Le Monde Informatique, Telecoms & Reseaux; **GERMANY's** Computerwoche, Computerwoche Focus, Computerwoche Extra, Computerwoche Karriere, Information Management, Macwelt, Netzwelt, PC Welt, PC Woche, Publish, Unit; **HUNGARY's** Alaplap, Computerworld SZT, PC World, ; **INDIA's** Computers & Communications; **ISRAEL's** Computerworld Israel, PC World Israel; **ITALY's** Computerworld Italia, Lotus Magazine, Macworld Italia, Networking Italia, PC World Italia; **JAPAN's** Computerworld Japan, Macworld Japan, SunWorld Japan, Windows World; **KENYA's** East African Computer News; **KOREA's** Computerworld Korea, Macworld Korea, PC World Korea; **MEXICO's** Compu Edicion, Compu Manufactura, Computacion/Punto de Venta, Computerworld Mexico, MacWorld, Mundo Unix, PC World, Windows; **THE NETHERLAND'S** Computer! Totaal, LAN Magazine, MacWorld; **NEW ZEALAND's** Computer Listings, Computerworld New Zealand, New Zealand PC World; **NIGERIA's** PC World Africa; **NORWAY's** Computerworld Norge, C/World, Lotusworld Norge, Macworld Norge, Networld, PC World Ekspress, PC World Norge, PC World's Product Guide, Publish World, Student Data, Unix World, Windowsworld, IDG Direct Response; **PANAMA's** PC World; **PERU's** Computerworld Peru, PC World; **PEOPLES REPUBLIC OF CHINA's** China Computerworld, PC World China, Electronics International, China Network World; **IDG HIGH TECH BEIJING's** New Product World; **IDG SHENZHEN's** Computer News Digest; **PHILLIPPINES'** Computerworld, PC World; **POLAND's** Computerworld Poland, PC World/Komputer; **PORTUGAL's** Cerebro/PC World, Correio Informatico/Computerworld, MacIn; **ROMANIA's** PC World; **RUSSIA's** Computerworld-Moscow, Mir-PC, Sety; **SLOVENIA's** Monitor Magazine; **SOUTH AFRICA's** Computing S.A.; **SPAIN's** Amiga World, Computerworld Espana, Communicaciones World, Macworld Espana, NeXTWORLD, PC World Espana, Publish, Sunworld; **SWEDEN's** Attack, ComputerSweden, Corporate Computing, Lokala Natverk/LAN, Lotus World, MAC&PC, Macworld, Mikrodatorn, PC World, Publishing & Design (CAP), Datalngenjoren, Maxi Data, Windows World; **SWITZERLAND's** Computerworld Schweiz, Macworld Schweiz, PC & Workstation; **TAIWAN's** Computerworld Taiwan, Global Computer Express, PC World Taiwan; **THAILAND's** Thai Computerworld; **TURKEY's** Computerworld Monitor, Macworld Turkiye, PC World Turkiye; **UNITED KINGDOM's** Lotus Magazine, Macworld, Sunworld; **UNITED STATES'** AmigaWorld, Cable in the Classroom, CD Review, CIO, Computerworld, Desktop Video World, DOS Resource Guide, Electronic News, Federal Computer Week, Federal Integrator, GamePro, IDG Books, InfoWorld, InfoWorld Direct, Laser Event, Macworld, Multimedia World, Network World, NeXTWORLD, PC Games, PC Letter, PC World Publish, Sumeria, SunWorld, SWATPro, Video Event; **VENEZUELA's** Computerworld Venezuela, MicroComputerworld Venezuela; **VIETNAM's** PC World Vietnam

Conventions

When you have to type something, it appears like this:

```
terribly important UNIX command
```

Be sure to type it just as it appears. Use the same capitalization we do, because UNIX considers the capital and small versions of the same letter to be totally different beasts. Then press the Enter or Return key.

In the text, UNIX commands and filenames are shown `in this typeface`.

Part II contains a cryptic "UNIXspeak" version of each command that shows all its options and arguments. Information in **bold** is required when you're using the command. Stuff in [square brackets] is optional, so try leaving it out. Text in *italics* represents information you provide: if you see *filename*, for example, fill in the name of the file you want to work with. Don't worry, we explain it all.

Contents at a Glance

Introduction

At last — a UNIX reference book that includes only the commands and options you might conceivably have some interest in! In this book, you will find information about lots of UNIX commands — more than 100 — and how to use them, but we have left out the other 10 zillion commands options that only nerds love.

We have also included information about several widely used parts of UNIX: the Motif window manager; the ed, vi, and emacs text editors; electronic mail; and networking. Don't flip through lots of different, confusing manuals to find that command you are looking for — just check out the relevant part of this book.

How to find things in this book

This book is divided into six sections so that you can find things fast.

Part I, "Using the Shell," has information about how to type commands, name files and directories, and use pipes and filters.

Part II, "UNIX Commands," contains our favorite 100 or so UNIX commands, with the options you are likely to use. We have included examples and warnings when necessary.

Part III, "Using Motif," was written for people who use UNIX's most popular window manager.

Part IV, "Using Text Editors," contains command summaries for the ed, vi, and emacs editors.

Part V, "Sending and Receiving Mail," has instructions for using the elm and mail programs to handle your electronic mail.

Part VI, "The Network," contains commands for accessing computers on a network.

The cast of icons

For each command we describe — and whenever we provide other important information — we include icons that tell you about what you are reading.

Recommended for your average UNIX user.

 Not recommended for your average UNIX user.

 Not suitable for your average UNIX user, but you may have to use it anyway.

 You can't do any real damage with this command.

 Useful, but you could do some damage by accident.

 Potentially dangerous but sometimes necessary. Try to stay away from this command, or get a UNIX wizard to review what you plan to do before you do it.

 A tip that can save you time or impress your local UNIX guru.

 Watch out! Something about this command or task can make trouble for you.

 A command or task that is useful if your computer is connected to a network. If not, don't use it!

 A handy cross-reference to the sections in *UNIX For Dummies* that cover this topic in more detail.

 A command that doesn't work in BSD UNIX. If you use UNIX System V, you are in luck.

 A command that works only in BSD UNIX. If you use UNIX System V, skip this command.

Part 1

Using the Shell

We start from the outside in, so the shell sounds like a good place to begin. (If this statement makes you think that UNIX resembles an insect, only not as attractive, we think along the same lines.) The *shell* is the program that reads your commands and does something with them. (How's that for precise technical language?) Six different shells are lurking around, but for the most part, they do the same thing.

Unless you're the victim — er, beneficiary — of a Fancy Windowed Graphical User Interface, the only way to get UNIX to do something is to type commands at it. Here, we discuss what commands look like and some general rules that apply to all commands. Even if you have an FWGUI, you will end up typing shell commands into a window, so you need some shell smarts anyway. (To use the most popular FWGUI — Motif — see Part III.)

The shell prompt

The shell tells you that it's ready for you to type a command by displaying a prompt string, usually a percent sign (%) for the C shell and a dollar sign ($) for the other shells. Some systems are set up with more complex prompts, including the terminal name, directory name, phase of the moon, and other junk.

Typing commands

Commands consist of a series of words, followed by pressing the Enter (or Return) key. The first word is the name of the command, and the res are *arguments* that affect the way the command works. If the command to remove a file is rm, for example, the arguments specify which file to remove. One space between words is plenty, although more won't hurt. Upper- and lowercase letters definitely do matter. All standard UNIX command names are lowercase, so you generally type commands in lowercase.

More stuff

Commands can be as long as you want. If you type a command that doesn't fit on a line, just keep typing and UNIX will continue it on the next line. It may look like two lines on your screen, but until you press Enter, the computer thinks that it's one line.

For more information about typing shell commands, see "Finally! You're Ready to Work" in Chapter 2 of *UNIX For Dummies*.

Special characters and what they do

Nearly every punctuation character means something special to the shell. Unfortunately, the exact characters vary from one system to another. (You can use the `stty` command to change these characters; see the entry for `stty` in Part II.) This section presents a roundup of the most useful special characters.

Character	What It Does
Enter or Return	Ends a line you're typing.
Space or Tab	Separates words in commands.
Backspace, Delete, or Ctrl-H	Backspaces over errors . If none of those characters works, try # (and use `stty` to change it to something else, if you prefer).
;	Separates two commands on the same line. Whoopee.
&	After a command, tells the shell to run that command in the background and return immediately for another command. (See `bg`, `fg`, and `kill` in Section II for commands to control background programs.) A pair of ampersands (&&) is an obscure way to perform the command following the && only if the one preceding the && succeeded.
|	Between two commands, splices the output of the first command to the input of the second, creating a pipeline (see the section "Redirection: pipes and filters" later in this part). A pair of vertical bars (||) is an obscure way to perform the command following the || only if the one preceding the || failed.

Special characters and what they do 5

Character	What It Does
!	In the C shell only, repeats a previously typed command, identified by what follows the !. Other than ! !, which repeats the preceding command, avoid exclamation points.
#	Whatever follows is a comment the shell ignores.
\	At the end of a line, indicates that the command is continued on the next line. Anywhere else, "quotes" the following character so that it isn't treated as a special character (see the section "Quoting characters on the command line" later in this part).
' or "	"Quotes" a group of characters so that they aren't treated as special characters (see "Quoting characters on the command line" later in this part).
$	Introduces a reference to a variable. See "Shell variables and the environment" later in this part.
?, *, and [ ]	Wildcard characters (see the "Wildcards" section later in this part).
( )	In the Korn and Bourne shells, group together commands you want to treat as a single command. They're kind of obscure and are used most often for redirecting the output of a bunch of commands (see the section "Redirection: pipes and filters," later in this part). On second thought, forget about them.
{ }	In the Bourne and Korn shells, group commands sort of like parentheses. Not widely used, except maybe in shell scripts.
Ctrl-C	Stops programs that are stuck. If possible, use the program's exit command or the equivalent. Some programs, particularly text editors, catch Ctrl-C and wait for you to type another command to the program. You can also try pressing the Delete key, if it doesn't work as a backspace.
Ctrl-D	Marks the end of input when you're typing directly to a program.
Ctrl-U or Ctrl-X	Cancels the line you're typing and starts over. If neither of those works, try @ (and use stty to change it to something more friendly).
Ctrl-Z	Pauses the program you're running. Then use the shell commands fg, bg, and kill to restart or stop them. Your shell has to know how to handle Ctrl-Z; some older shells don't. (See the entries for the fg, bg, and kill commands in Part II.)

More stuff

If you don't want to remember all this punctuation glop, just don't use special characters in your shell commands! To use them in commands as though they were normal characters, "quote" them (see "Quoting characters on the command line" later in this part).

Most shells interpret Ctrl-D as a command to log you out. So don't press it when you see the shell prompt. To terminate the program you're running, try Ctrl-C or Delete (if that's not backspace).

Even though your keyboard has arrow keys and the cursor moves as it should when you press them, the only UNIX programs that understand them are full-screen text editors. Anywhere else, they produce useless junk like ^[[A^[[D^[[B^[[C.

Don't confuse the Backspace key, which usually works everywhere, with the left arrow key, which works only in full-screen editors.

For information about using Ctrl-Z, see the section "The Magic of Job Control" in Chapter 15 of *UNIX For Dummies*.

Filenames

Permanently stored information in UNIX is stored in files. Each file has a name (each one can have many names, in fact, but we'll worry about that later — see the ln entry in Part II).

You can use letters, digits, periods, hyphens, and underscores in your names. (You can use other characters as well, but stick to these to avoid confusion.) Upper- and lowercase are different, so tadpole, TadPole, and TADPOLE are three different filenames.

Don't use weird characters in filenames, such as any of these:

/ ! @ # $ ^ & * - ( ) + ' " \ / ?

Also, don't use spaces in filenames. Most programs don't let you anyway. Use periods or underlines to string words together.

Directories

A *directory* is a special kind of file that contains the names of other files. All UNIX files are arranged in directories.

At any given moment, one directory is your *current directory* (or *working directory)* of files you are using right now. When you first log in, your current directory is your *home directory* (or *login directory),* which the system administrator made for you.

You can — and usually should — make other directories in which to store files for various projects. You can switch to other directories with the chdir or cd command, make new directories with mkdir, and get rid of directories you no longer want with rmdir. (See the entries for these commands in Part II.)

More stuff

In the C and Korn shells, the name ~ (tilde) is shorthand for your home directory. If your home directory is /usr/elvis, therefore, ~/hits is the same as /usr/elvis/hits.

See "What Is a Directory?" in Chapter 5 of *UNIX For Dummies*.

As with filenames, you can use upper- and lowercase letters, digits, periods, hyphens, and underscores in your directory names. Upper- and lowercase are different.

A good rule of thumb is to use all lowercase for files and use initial capital letters for directories.

Pathnames

A *pathname* tells UNIX how to find the particular file you want. If you use a plain filename (tadpole, for example), UNIX understands it as a file in the current directory. You refer to files in other directories by using a list of names strung together with slashes. The name snacks/tadpole means to look in the current directory for a subdirectory called snacks, and for a file called tadpole. This system can be carried to unhealthy lengths:

```
snacks/vertebrate/green/crunchy/wiggly/tadpole
```

If the path begins with a slash, it's an *absolute path*, one that starts from the "root" of the file system. A typical absolute path is /usr/elvis/songs/hound_dog. An absolute path always means the same thing regardless of what your current directory is.

See "Divide and Conquer" in Chapter 5 of *UNIX For Dummies*.

Wildcards

Often, you want to have a command operate on a group of files with similar names. The shell lets you use special "wildcard characters" to specify a group of files. This list shows the three primary kinds of wildcards:

Character	What It Does
?	Matches any single character
*	Matches any number of characters
[ ]	Matches any one of the letters in the brackets

More stuff

For example, h* indicates all the files in the current directory that begin with an *h*; h*g indicates all the files that begin with *h* and end with *g*; part[123] indicates files named *part1*, *part2*, and *part3*; part[0-9] indicates all of *part0* through *part9*; and * indicates every file in the directory.

Unlike some cheesy PC systems, UNIX wildcards do the right thing even when you use directories. For example, */*c means all files that end with the letter *c* in subdirectories of the current directory.

Wildcards are handled by the shell itself, not by the command you are running. The good news is that all commands handle wildcards in exactly the same way; you don't have to remember that some do or some don't. The bad news is that even when part of a command isn't a filename, if it has stars or question marks or brackets, the shell tries to make filenames out of it unless you quote it (see "Quoting characters on the command line" later in this part).

It's not always easy to know how wildcards will work. Before doing something dangerous with them, such as deleting a bunch files, use the ls command to see which filenames your wildcards match.

See "Wild and Crazy Wildcards" in Chapter 6 of *UNIX For Dummies*.

Quoting characters on the command line

Sometimes you have to use special characters in your commands. For example, to list filenames that have a question mark in them, you need to tell the shell that the question mark you are typing should *not* be interpreted as a wildcard character. This is called *quoting* the character. You can quote any single special character, including a space, by preceding it with a backslash (\). You can even type \\ to quote a backslash. For example, this command lists filenames that contain a question mark:

```
ls *\?*
```

More stuff

Single and double quotation marks quote strings of characters. They must match correctly. Single quotes are somewhat more "potent" than double quotes. Everything between double quotes is taken literally, even backslashes, with the following caveats:

- Wildcard characters (such as * and ?) are taken literally, that is, they don't match groups of filenames.

- Dollar-sign variable names are replaced by their values.

- You can quote double quotes in single quotes and vice versa. (Say that three times fast.)

To display the text `"Too #&@!;) much punctuation!"` on-screen, you can use `echo` like this:

```
echo "Too #&@!;) much punctuation!"
```

If the last character on a line is a backslash, it means that the command continues on the next line.

Redirection: pipes and filters

Every UNIX command has *standard input* and *standard output*. Both are normally the terminal. You can tell the shell to redirect the input or output of any command.

Character	What It Does
>	Redirects output of a command to a file or device.
>>	Redirects the output of a command, adding it to the existing file if there is one.
<	Redirects input of command from a file or device.
|	Sends ("pipes") the output of one command to become the input of another command.

More stuff

For example, to store a listing of files into `myfiles`, type this line:

```
ls -l > myfiles
```

To append the listing to the end of an existing file:

```
ls -l >> myfiles
```

To sort the contents of the file `mydata` and send the results to the screen:

```
sort < mydata
```

To sort `mydata` and produce `mysorteddata`:

```
sort < mydata > mysorteddata
```

You can redirect the output of one program into the input of another by using a *pipe*, which is written as a vertical bar (|). To make a file listing and send it to the printer:

```
ls -l | lpr
```

You can pipe together as many programs as you want. To make a file listing, add headings with `pr`, and print the result:

```
ls -l | pr -h "my files" | lpr
```

Programs that are usually used with redirection are called *filters*. The filters you are most likely to run into are `more`, `sort`, and maybe `tee` (see their entries in Part II).

See "This Output Is Going To Havana: Redirection" and "Gurgle, Gurgle: Running Data Through Pipes" in Chapter 6 of *UNIX For Dummies*.

Which shell am I using?

To figure out which shell you're using, type the following line:

```
echo $RANDOM
```

and then press the Enter key. If you get a blank line, it's the *Bourne shell*. If you get the following line:

```
RANDOM: Undefined variable
```

it's the *C shell*. If you get a 5-digit random number, it's the *Korn Shell*.

See the section "Cracking the Shell" in Chapter 2 of *UNIX For Dummies*.

Part II

UNIX Commands

Yuck — commands! If it weren't for commands, UNIX wouldn't be that hard to use, really. But `grep`? `awk`? These words don't look like commands — they look like intestinal noises!

If you use UNIX, however, you have to use UNIX commands. UNIX has zillions of them, and we have selected just the ones that meet one of these criteria:

- You might want to use it yourself
- A UNIX expert (also known as a *guru*) might tell you to use it

Either way, you have to know how they work, what to type, and which mistakes to avoid. This part of the book lists the most useful UNIX commands, along with the options and arguments they expect. Oops — sorry about that jargon. *Options* and *arguments* are the information you type on the command line, right after you type the command. Some commands can work in 17 different ways, depending on the options you use, so we tell you about just the ones you are likely to run into.

We also include cute little icons to tell you which types of UNIX the command works with, whether it's safe to use (whether it's likely to erase your disk), and how likely you are to have it. (All the icons and their meanings are listed in the Introduction of this book.)

For each command, we include a "UNIXspeak" section, showing all the options and arguments you might have to use. In this section, information in **bold** is required when you're using the command. Stuff in [square brackets] is optional, so you can usually leave it out. Text in *italics* represents information you provide: for example, where you see *filename*, you fill in the name of the file you want to work with (don't type "filename"!).

alias

C and Korn shells only.

Creates an alias for a command or shows which aliases exist.

UNIXspeak (C shell)

alias [*name* ['*command*']]

UNIXspeak (Korn shell)

alias [*name*=['*command*']]

Option or Argument	Function
name	Specifies the alias name
command	Specifies the command the name should be an alias for

Sample

You are sick of typing a long UNIX command you use often. Instead, you want to assign it a short nickname, or *alias*, which is faster to type. You are tired of typing ls -l, for example, and would rather just type d to see the files in your directory.

If you use the C shell, you type

```
alias d 'ls -l'
```

If you use the Korn shell, you type

```
alias d='ls -l'
```

Either way, you have just created a new command, d, which is the same as ls -l. This command is cool, although the next time you log in, UNIX will have forgotten all about this alias.

More stuff

To see which aliases you have defined, just type

```
alias
```

See the section "Using an alias" in Chapter 14 of *UNIX For Dummies*. To make an alias permanent, talk to a UNIX wizard about putting this alias command into your .profile or .login file (any wizard worth her salt knows what this statement means). Or see the instructions in the section "Do I Have to Type the Same Things Every Time I Log In?" in Chapter 28 of *UNIX For Dummies*.

at

Schedules a command to be run at a particular time. This command is great for running time-consuming commands later, such as in the middle of the night.

UNIXspeak

at [-f *filename*] [-m] ***time*** [*date*]

or

at -l

or

at -r *job*

Option or Argument	Function
-f *filename*	Specifies the name of the file that contains the command (or commands) to run.
-m	Sends you an electronic-mail message after the command has been run.
time	Indicates when you want the command to run. You type the time in the format *hh:mm* followed by **am** or **pm**, or you can use a 24-hour clock. You can type **midnight** to run your command at night or **now** + followed by the number of minutes or hours (for example, **now + 6 hours**).
date	Indicates on which day you want the command to run. You type the date in the format *month day, year*, where *month* is the name of the month (such as **Dec** or **December**, not 12), *day* is the day (such as **25**), and *year* is the four-digit year (such as **1994**). You need the year only if the date is more than 12 months in the future. (We've heard of planning ahead, but that's ridiculous!)
-l	Lists the names of commands (jobs) you have already scheduled. Don't type anything on the command line after -l.

Option or Argument	Function
-r *job*	Cancels a command (job) you previously scheduled. On the command line, type the *job* number after -r. To find out the job number, use the -l option we just described.

Sample

You want to print a huge document during the night. (You don't want to tie up the printer because you are the soul of consideration.) You type

```
at midnight
```

After you press Enter, UNIX doesn't display a prompt. Instead, it waits for you to type the command (or commands) you want to run at midnight. You type

```
lpr big.report
```

After pressing Enter again, you press Ctrl-D to tell UNIX that you are finished typing commands for at to schedule. Now you have scheduled a "job!"

More stuff

After you have scheduled a job, you can check that at hasn't forgotten about it. You type

```
at -l
```

You see a list of your scheduled jobs, with their job numbers. If you decide to cancel one (for example, the job whose number is 753460300.a), you type

```
at -r 753460300.a
```

Your system administrator can control who is allowed to use at and who isn't. If you're not on the list, at tells you when you try to use it, so you have to see whether you can talk your way on to the list.

For more information, see the section "Time Is Money — Steal Some Today!" in Chapter 13 of *UNIX For Dummies*.

awk

A strange programming language used by UNIX nerds to perform an amazing array of tasks.

UNIXspeak

awk -f *program file*

Option or Argument	Function
program	Specifies the name of the awk program to run (don't even think about learning to write them yourself, unless you want to become a nerd)
file	Specifies the name of the file you want to modify by using the awk program, or that serves as input to it

Sample

Programs written in awk usually read one file (the input) and create another file (the output). If you keep your checkbook in a file, for example, one check to a line, it's easy (easy for awk nerds, anyway) to whip up a program to compute the current balance.

More stuff

Other versions of awk are named gawk and nawk. They all work more or less the same. If you want to create your own awk programs, read a good book about it, such as O'Reilly & Associates' *sed & awk* (by Dale Dougherty).

---

bc

A handy-dandy desk calculator.

UNIXspeak

bc [*file*]

Option or Argument	Function
file	Specifies the name of a file full of bc commands. If you want to multiply just a few numbers, leave out this option.

Sample

You have just talked your boss into spending $5,000 on a beautiful UNIX workstation for you. After you install it, she stops by your desk to talk about budgets, and you have to add up a few figures. Imagine how embarrassed you would be if your expensive new toy couldn't sum a few numbers! No problem — you type

    bc

UNIX, in its usual taciturn way, says nothing. You type

    4500 * .67

to calculate a quick discount. Whew! bc displays the answer. When you are finished doing calculations, you press Ctrl-D or type

    quit

More stuff

The bc calculator can do an unbelievable number of computations, including square roots, trigonometry, and conditional calculations, and converting between hexadecimal, octal, and decimal numbers, all to hundreds or thousands of digits. You can even define your own functions. On the other hand, when was the last time you needed the cosine of something?

See the section "A Desk Calculator" in Chapter 13 of *UNIX For Dummies*.

---

bg

Continues a stopped job in the background. (Some older versions of the Bourne and Korn shells cannot do this.)

UNIXspeak

> **bg** [*job*]

Option or Argument	Function
job	Specifies the job number you want to run in the background. If you leave it out, UNIX assumes that you mean the current job.

Sample

You start a big, slow program and then realize that you want to run it in the background so that you can get some other work done in the meantime. You press Ctrl-Z to stop the job. UNIX says something like Stopped. To continue the job in the background and leave the foreground free for you to give other commands, you type

    bg

More stuff

To find out which jobs are running in the background, you type

    jobs

To cancel a job that is running in the background, you use the kill command. To move a background into the foreground, you use the fg command. (Both are described later in this part of the book.)

 Some versions of the Bourne and Korn shells don't have *job control*, which is the capability to run jobs in the background. If pressing Ctrl-Z doesn't stop a job, your shell doesn't have it. Bummer.

 See the section "The Magic of Job Control" in Chapter 15 of *UNIX For Dummies*.

---

cal

Prints a calendar for a month or a year.

UNIXspeak

cal [*month*] [*year*]

Option or Argument	Function
month	Specifies the month (1 to 12) for which you want a calendar
year	Specifies the year (1 to 9999) for which you want a calendar

Sample

You are planning a big trip down the Amazon for next March and your desk calendar doesn't go that far into the future. You type

```
cal 3 1995
```

More stuff

If you type just `cal` with no month or year, you get the calendar for the current month. If you provide a year but no month, `cal` prints a 12-month calendar for the year. And yes, it can print a calendar for the year 1, if you want it (that's 1 A.D.!).

To save the calendar in a text file rather than print it on-screen, redirect `cal`'s output to a file, like this:

```
cal 12 1995 > xmas.trip.calendar
```

Because `cal` can do calendars back to the year 1, typing `cal 95` prints a calendar for the year 95 A.D., not 1995, so watch out.

See the section "Calendar Games" in Chapter 13 of *UNIX For Dummies*.

calendar

Displays appointments and reminders for today.

UNIXspeak

```
calendar
```

Sample

To use the `calendar` program, you first need a `calendar` file. Use any text editor to create a file named `calendar` in your home directory. In it, you type appointments, reminders, and snide remarks, along with the date on which you want them displayed. Here is a sample `calendar` file:

```
nov 5 Send invitations for Meg's birthday party
nov 20  Bought decorations for Meg's birthday
        party yet?
11/30 Get Meg a present!
12/4 Meg's birthday party at 11AM!
```

When you run the `calendar` program, it displays any lines that begin with today's date. To display calendar reminders every day when you log in, add this line to the end of your `.login` or `.profile` file:

```
calendar
```

When you log in on November 30, you see this message:

```
11/30 Get Meg a present!
```

More stuff

If you use electronic mail (see `mail` or `elm`), you don't have to run the `calendar` program. If you have a file named `calendar` in your home directory, UNIX automagically runs the `calendar` every day at midnight and mails you the resulting messages. When you arrive in the morning, your reminders are in your mailbox. Pretty cute!

See the section "Calendar Games" in Chapter 13 of *UNIX For Dummies.*

cancel

Cancels a print job (UNIX System V only).

UNIXspeak

cancel *requestID*

Option or Argument	Function
requestID	Specifies the print job you want to cancel, by using the request ID number listed by the `lpstat` command (described later in this part of the book)

Sample

You send a large report to the printer. Looking carefully at your word processor, you see that the footer is wrong and that every single page is therefore messed up. To cancel the print job, you first find out its request ID by typing

```
lpstat
```

UNIX responds with a listing like this:

```
lj-1756 margyl 94832 Jan 12 10:43 on lj
lj-1762 margyl 1298 Jan 12 10:45 on lj
```

The first line describes the print job you want to cancel (you can tell because its size, 94,832 characters, is big). You type

```
cancel lj-1756
```

UNIX responds

```
request "lj-1756" canceled
```

More stuff

You can skip using `lpstat` if the job you want to cancel is printing. Instead, you can just specify the name of the printer, like this:

```
cancel lj
```

This line cancels whatever job is printing on the printer named `lj`.

If you use BSD UNIX, see `lprm`.

See the section "Cancel the order, System V" in Chapter 9 of *UNIX For Dummies*.

---

cat

Displays a file on the screen.

UNIXspeak

cat *filename*

Option or Argument	Function
filename	Specifies the name of the file you want to see

Sample

You see a rather interesting file in your boss's directory. Not that you are nosy or anything, but you wonder what's in it. You type

```
cat bonus.plan
```

More stuff

cat works fine for text files, but other types of files look like hieroglyphics. To peek in other kinds of files, you have to know which program creates or interprets them — to look at a word processing document, for example, you have to use the word processor.

If the file you want to look at is long, use the more command instead.

You can also use the cat command (which stands for catenate, if you care) to combine two or more files, like this:

```
cat file1 file2 file3 > one.big.file
```

See the section "Looking at the Guts of a File" in Chapter 4, the section "The cat and the fiddle, er, file" in Chapter 6, the section "COPY A + B C" in Chapter 16, and the section "The cat Command" in Chapter 29 of *UNIX For Dummies*.

cd

Changes to another directory (changes the current working directory to the directory you indicate).

UNIXspeak

cd [*directory*]

Option or Argument	Function
directory	Specifies the directory to which you want to move. This directory becomes your current working directory. If you leave this option out, you move to your own home directory.

Sample

You log in and do some work in your home directory. Next, you want to move into your budget directory to see which files are there. You type

```
cd budget
```

To move back up to the parent directory of budget, you type

```
cd ..
```

More stuff

To move back to your home directory, type

```
cd
```

To move to a directory that is not a subdirectory of the current working directory, you can use a full pathname, one that begins with a slash. To look around in the /usr directory (where all home directories are stored), for example, you can type

```
cd /usr
```

If you use the Korn shell, this command moves to the last directory you were in, as shown in the following line:

```
cd -
```

See the section "I've been working in the directory" in Chapter 5 and the section "The cd Command" in Chapter 29 of *UNIX For Dummies*.

---

chgrp

Changes the group that has access to a file or directory (System V only).

UNIXspeak

```
chgrp newgroup filenames
```

Option or Argument	Function
newgroup	Specifies the name of the group that assumes ownership of the file (or files)
filenames	Specifies the files to change

Sample

You have just finished creating a form to be used by your organization's accounting department. To enable them to use it, you want to change ownership of the file from your group to the acctg group. You type

```
chgrp acctg snazzy.form
```

More stuff

You have to own the file or directory to use this command. To change the group ownership of a bunch of files at the same time, you can use a wildcard in the filename.

If you use BSD UNIX, you must ask your system administrator to change the group to which a file belongs.

See the section "File seeks new group; can sing, dance, and do tricks" in Chapter 28 of *UNIX For Dummies*.

chmod

Changes the permissions for a file.

UNIXspeak

chmod [-R] *permissions filenames*

Option or Argument	Function
-R	Tells chmod to change permissions on files in subdirectories too.
permissions	Specifies the permissions (also called the *mode*) to assign to the file (or files). Permissions consist of a letter that tells who gets the permission, a character that indicates whether to add (+) or remove (-) the permission, and a letter that tells which kind of permission.
filenames	Specifies the file (or files) to change.

Who Gets the Permission

Code	Who
u	User who owns the file
g	Group that owns the file
o	Other (everyone else)
a	All (everybody)

Which Kind of Permission

Code	Which Kind
r	Read the file
w	Write or edit the file
x	Execute (run) the file as a program

Sample

You create a shell script and now you want to be able to execute it. You type

```
chmod a+x newscript
```

This line allows everyone to execute the script.

Or you write a memo criticizing the top management of your organization and stating your intention to quit and take a job with a competitor. On reflection, you decide that it would be better if the text of the memo didn't leak out before your meeting with the big boss. To prevent others from reading it, you type

```
chmod go-r last.memo
```

More stuff

You have to own the file or directory to use this command.

If you leave the "who" letter out of the permission, chmod assigns the permission to everyone.

Some heavy-duty UNIX nerds use numeric permission codes rather than the letter codes we favor. If someone tells you to set a file's permission to 440 or some other number, just ask for an English translation.

See the section "A bin of shells" in Chapter 14 and the section "If Mom says no, ask Dad" in Chapter 28 of *UNIX For Dummies.*

chown

Changes the owner of a file (System V only).

UNIXspeak

chown [-R] *newowner filenames*

Option or Argument	Function
-R	Tells chown to change the ownership of files in subdirectories too.
newowner	Specifies the name of the new owner of the file (the current owner must be you or else the command doesn't work). Use the person's UNIX username.
filenames	Specifies the file (or files) to change.

Sample

You have written a report and now you want to pass it along to Helen, who will finish it up. After moving the file to Helen's home directory, you type

```
chown helen final.report
```

Now Helen owns the file.

More stuff

You have to own the file to be able to use this command. If you want to give a file to someone else, you might think that it would be enough to copy it to the person's home directory. To give the person permissions to fool with the file, however, it's best to change the file's ownership. After all, you can always keep a copy.

Another way to create a file with a different owner is for the new owner to copy the file. Helen could make a copy of your report, for example. If she performs the `cp` command, she owns the copy. You just have to give her read permission for the file (see `chmod`).

See the section "Finding a new owner" in Chapter 28 of *UNIX For Dummies*.

clear

Clears the screen.

UNIXspeak

```
clear
```

Sample

You have just tried to use the `cat` command to look at a word-processing document and your screen is full of gibberish, which is giving you a headache. You type

```
clear
```

Aah. . . .

More stuff

This command doesn't affect files or jobs — it just clears the clutter from your screen.

cmp

Compares two files and tells you the line numbers where they differ.

UNIXspeak

cmp *onefile anotherfile*

Option or Argument	Function
onefile	Specifies the name of one of the files to compare
anotherfile	Specifies the name of the other file to compare

Sample

You have two versions of a letter you have written and you cannot tell which is the final version. You type

cmp letter.to.dad letter.to.daddy

If UNIX says nothing, the two letters are exactly the same, character for character. Otherwise, UNIX tells you how far it got into the file before it found something different.

More stuff

The problem with cmp is that it doesn't show you what's different about the files. For text files, you get far more information by using diff. On the other hand, it cannot work with nontext files, and cmp can.

See the section "Comparing Apples and Oranges" in Chapter 13 of *UNIX For Dummies*.

compress

Shrinks a file into one "compressed" file so that it takes up less space on your disk.

UNIXspeak

compress [-v] *filenames*

Option or Argument	Function
-v	Displays how much the file (or files) shrank
filenames	Specifies the file (or files) to compress

Sample

You have finished writing your magnum opus and have mailed the manuscript to the publisher. You want to save all your manuscript files (named chapter1, chapter2, and so on) in a compressed format to save space. You type

```
compress -v chapter*
```

compress creates compressed files named chapter1.Z, chapter2.Z, and so on that contain freeze-dried versions of each chapter. It also deletes the original files.

More stuff

When you want to get your original files back, you use uncompress or zcat (described later in this part of the book).

It's a good idea to compress your files before transferring them over the network to another computer. The smaller the file, the faster it transfers. If you want one big, compressed file, create a combined file by using ar and compress the combined file.

See also pack, unpack, and pcat.

See the section "Squashing Your Files" in Chapter 13 of *UNIX For Dummies*.

cp

Copies one or more files.

UNIXspeak

cp [-i] ***oldfiles newfiles***

or

cp [-i] [-r] ***oldfiles directory***[/newfiles]

Option or Argument	Function
-i	Ask first, before you replace an existing file with a copied file (works only in UNIX System V Release 4)
-r	When you copy a directory, it copies its subdirectories too and creates new subdirectories as necessary
oldfiles	Specifies the name of the file you want to copy
newfiles	Specifies the name to give to the new copy
directory	Specifies the name of the directory in which you want to store a copy

Sample

You have a file that contains your January expense report. Rather than create your February expense report from scratch, you want to begin with a copy of the one for January. You type

```
cp january.expenses february.expenses
```

UNIX doesn't change the contents of `january.expenses` in any way — it just creates a new file called `february.expenses` with identical contents.

If you want to copy your finished `february.expenses` file into your boss's home directory, you type

```
cp february.expenses /usr/harold/ margys.feb.expenses
```

By including both a path and a filename to which to copy, you tell `cp` to copy the file into the `/usr/harold/` directory and to name the new copy `margys.feb.expenses`.

More stuff

If you know DOS, you might think that omitting the second filename tells `cp` to copy a file into the current working directory. This technique doesn't work in UNIX — instead, use a period (.) to copy a file into the current directory.

What happens if you copy a file to a new name and a file already has that name? Blammo! — that's what happens. Assuming that you have permission to write (change) the existing file, UNIX blows it away and replaces it with the copied file. Always use the `ls` command to check that your new filename isn't already in use. And use the `-i` option to tell `cp` to ask first before whomping a file.

See the section "Copying Files: Send In the Clones" in Chapter 4 and the section "The cp Command" in Chapter 29 of *UNIX For Dummies*.

cpio

Creates and uncreates *cpio format* archive files. Also copies files to and from things other than hard disks.

UNIXspeak

cpio -i [-c] [-d] [-E *listname*] [-u] [-v] [-V] [*filenames*]

or

cpio -o [-c] [-v] [-V]

or

cpio -p [-d] [-l] -[u] [-v] [-V] *directory*

Option or Argument	Function
-c	Reads and writes archives in portable character format rather than in unportable binary format
-d	Creates directories as necessary; doesn't work with -o
-E	Specifies that a file contains a list of filenames to be copied; doesn't work with -o or -p
-i	Specifies that cpio copy the files from another device (usually a tape) or an archive file back to the disk
-l	Creates links to the files, if possible, rather than copies them; doesn't work with -i or -o
-o	Specifies that cpio copy the files from the disk to another device (usually a tape) or to an archive file
-p	Specifies that cpio copy the files from one directory to another on the disk

Option or Argument	Function
-u	Copies files even if it means replacing existing files with the same names (watch out!); doesn't work with ⁻o
-v	Displays a list of filenames as it copies them
-V	Displays a dot for each file it copies so that you can tell how fast it's going
listname	Specifies the name of a file that contains a list of files to copy; if you use this option, don't use *filenames*
filenames	Specifies the names of the files to be copied; if you use this option, don't use *listname*
directory	Specifies the name of the directory to which to copy the files

Sample

You have just finished a large project for which you created a bunch of files. You personally never want to see the files again, but you know that you should save them for posterity. To copy the files to an archive file, you type

```
cpio -oc proj.plan report.draft report.final >
proj.archive
```

This command creates an archive file named `proj.archive` that contains your project files.

Later, of course, it turns out that you have to make one or two little changes to your final report. To get the `report.final` file (and other files) back from the archive, you type

```
cpio -icd < proj.archive
```

More stuff

To move a bunch of files from one directory to another, including all the subdirectories, you may be able to use the `cp -r` command. If it doesn't work on your system, use the following magic incantation (it's ugly, but it's easier than any of the alternatives):

```
cd olddir
```

```
find * -print | cpio -pdlmv /usr/whatever/newdir
```

These commands move all the files from the `olddir` directory and its subdirectories to the `/usr/whatever/newdir` directory, creating new subdirectories as necessary. It sort of resembles grafting a limb from one tree to another.

Important: Specify the name of the new directory as a full pathname. The new directory must already exist. (Use mkdir to create it if necessary.) After this command has run, the files exist in both the old and new directories — use rm -r to get rid of the old directory. And yes, this technique is baroque.

The cpio command is used also for copying files to and from tapes, as part of a backup procedure. *See also* tar.

crontab

Makes a list of programs you want to run on a regular schedule.

UNIXspeak

crontab [*filename*]

Option or Argument	Function
filename	Specifies the file that contains the list of commands and when you want to run each one

To use crontab, you need a *crontab file:* this file contains a list of commands you want to run and the time and day when you want to run them. A crontab file is a text file, and each line of the file contains one command, like this:

```
min hour DOM month DOW command
```

The first five items specify when the command should be run, as described in this table:

Lines in a crontab file

Item	Description
min	Minute (0 to 59)
hour	Hour (0 to 23)
DOM	Day of the month (1 to 31)
month	Month (1 to 12)
DOW	Day of the week (0 to 6, where 0 is Sunday)
command	Command to run

Sample

You want to mail yourself a message every Friday to remind yourself to pick up groceries on the way home. You create a crontab file named `my.crontab.file` (using any text editor) that contains this line:

```
0 0 * * 5 echo "Pick up groceries!" | mail margy
```

This line indicates that at midnight (0 minute and 0 hour), regardless of the day of the month (*), in all months (*), on Fridays (day 5), to send a message to yourself by way of UNIX mail (this line assumes that your username is `margy`). To tell the `crontab` program to run this command regularly, you type

```
crontab <my.crontab.file
```

More stuff

You can use `crontab` only if your system administrator allows you to. Your system administrator can also check or cancel commands that you have scheduled. To see your current crontab file, use `crontab -l`.

---

csh

Runs the C shell, optionally running a script of stored commands.

UNIXspeak

csh [*scriptname*]

Sample

Someone gives you a shell script named `new.program` written for the C shell. To run it, you type

```
csh new.program
```

More stuff

When you use UNIX, you are always using a shell. The other shells are the Bourne shell (`sh`) and the Korn shell (`ksh`). The main time that normal people run `csh` themselves is to run a script of C shell commands that someone else wrote. But because it's nearly impossible to write a C shell script that works, most scripts are written for the Bourne shell (sh) or the Korn shell (ksh).

For a description of UNIX shells, see the section "Cracking the Shell" in Chapter 2 of *UNIX For Dummies*.

cu

Calls up another system.

UNIXspeak

    cu *systemname*

Option or Argument	Function
systemname	Specifies the name of the computer system you want to call over the phone

Sample

You want to call CompuServe to download some information. To use UNIX as a terminal, you type

    cu CompuServe

You type commands to CompuServe as usual. After you have logged off from CompuServe, you terminate cu by typing the following line on a line by itself:

    ~.

More stuff

For cu to work, your system administrator must have set up the modem, the phone line, and list of system names and phone numbers. If the modem and phone line are set up, but you want to call a system whose name is not on the list, you can type the phone number in place of the system name and omit all spaces and punctuation. For example, you can type

    cu 5551223

See the sidebar "Dialing out" in Chapter 20 of *UNIX For Dummies*.

date

Tells you the current date and time, taking into account your time zone and, if appropriate, daylight savings time.

UNIXspeak

```
date
```

Sample

You wonder what day it is. You type

```
date
```

UNIX clears up any confusion you might have by displaying something like this:

```
Mon Jan 4 15:56:32 EST 1994
```

More stuff

Far too many options let you control the exact format of the date display, but the one UNIX uses is usually clear enough. If you want to see only the date, for example, you type

```
date +"%D"
```

If you want only the time, you type

```
date +"%r"
```

True weenies stay up until 2:00 a.m. the last weekends in March and October to be sure that daylight time changes correctly.

df

Displays how much space is free on your disk.

UNIXspeak

```
df [-b] [directory]
```

Option or Argument	Function
-b	Displays only the amount of free space in kilobytes
directory	Displays space on the file system where that directory resides

Sample

You are wondering how much space is on the disk on which your home directory is stored. Assuming that your username is elvis, you type

```
df /usr/elvis
```

More stuff

On System V, the directory name must be given as an absolute path starting with a slash. On BSD, any directory name will do.

The df listing includes lots of information about each *file system* to which you have access, including its total size, the amount of space that is full (used), the free space, the percentage that is full (capacity), and, if it is a *mounted directory*, which file server it is on.

For information about mounted directories, see the section "The df command" in Chapter 19 of *UNIX For Dummies*.

---

diff

Compares two files and prints the lines in which the files differ.

UNIXspeak

diff [-b] [-i] [-w] *filename1 filename2*

or

diff [-b] [-i] [-w] *filename1 directory1*

or, for BSD UNIX only

diff [-b] [-i] [-r] [-w] *directory1 directory2*

Option or Argument	Function
-b	Treats groups of spaces (blanks) as single spaces, so it ignores spacing differences.
-i	Ignores the difference between uppercase and lowercase letters.
-r	When you're comparing two directories, specifies that subdirectories should be compared too.
-w	Ignores all spaces and tabs.

Option or Argument	Function
filename1	Specifies one file to compare.
filename2	Specifies the other file to compare.
directory1	Specifies one directory to compare. If you tell `diff` to compare a file to a directory, it looks in the directory for a file of the same name and compares the two files (BSD only).
directory2	Specifies the other directory to compare. If you tell `diff` to compare two directories, it looks in both directories for files of the same name and compares all pairs of files with the same names. It also lists the names of files that are in one directory but not in the other.

Sample

You and a friend have been collaborating on a book (a purely hypothetical example). You both have copies of the various chapters in subdirectories of your home directories. The files should be exactly the same, but are they? To compare them, you type

```
diff /usr/margy/book /usr/john/book
```

UNIX looks in the two directories and compares pairs of the files with the same names. For example, it compares the following files:

```
/usr/margy/book/chapter1 and /usr/john/book/chapter1
```

```
/usr/margy/book/chapter2 and /usr/john/book/chapter2
```

Whenever UNIX finds a difference, it prints the lines from both files, like this:

```
23c23
< was the largest chocolate cake she had ever seen.
- - -
< was the largest chocolate cake she had ever seen.
45a
> "More vanilla!" she said again.
62d
< The End
```

The report describes the differences by telling how to turn the first file into the second. `23c23` means that line 23 in the first file (it's listed beginning with a `<`) should be changed to line 23 in the second file (listed beginning with a >). 45a indicates that a line should be added at the new line 45, and 62d means that line 62 of the first file should be deleted.

More stuff

To compare two really big files, use bdiff instead. It works just like diff, only slower. To compare files that don't contain text, use cmp. *See also* cmp, dircmp, and sdiff.

 See the section "Comparing Apples and Oranges" in Chapter 13 of *UNIX For Dummies.*

---

dircmp

Compares two directories and tells you which files are in both, which are in just one, and which are in just the other. For files in both directories, the dircmp command tells you whether the contents of the files are the same.

UNIXspeak

dircmp [-d] [-s] *directory1 directory2*

Option or Argument	Function
-d	For files that are in both directories, compare them by using the diff command
-s	Doesn't say anything about files that are identical
directory1	Specifies one directory to compare
directory2	Specifies the other directory to compare

Sample

Both you and your boss have been keeping copies of your department's monthly reports. Each of you has a directory named Reports that contains a bunch of files, and they seem to be more or less the same. You wonder whether either one of you is missing any files or whether they all are exactly the same. You type

```
dircmp /usr/margy/Reports /usr/lydia/Reports
```

The result of dircmp tells you only whether files are identical. *See also* diff, which can also compare two directories and tell you exactly how files differ.

---

du

Tells you how much disk space your files occupy.

UNIXspeak

du [-a] [-s] *directories*

Option or Argument	Function
-a	Displays the space used by each file, not just by each directory
-s	Displays the total space used for each directory, but not subdirectories
directories	Specifies the directory or directories to include in the disk usage listing

Sample

Your system administrator complains that your files take up too much space on the disk. "Nonsense," you reply, but then you realize that it might be better not to make him angry. Instead, you decide to refute the accusation with cold, hard evidence. You type

```
du /usr/margy
```

You see

```
162 /usr/margy/games
1492 /usr/margy/book
5403 /usr/margy/gossip
8550 /usr/margy
```

More stuff

The size is reported in disk blocks, which are 512 characters (half a kilobyte) in UNIX System V and 1,024 (1 kilobyte) in BSD UNIX.

echo

Echoes back whatever you type on the command line after echo
and expands any wildcards by using *, ?, or [ ].

UNIXspeak

echo [-n] *stuff*

Option or Argument	Function
-n	Doesn't begin a new line after echoing the information (BSD only).
stuff	Specifies the information to echo. If it is more than one word or contains punctuation, enclose the message in quotes. Part I of this book, in the section "Quoting characters on the command line," contains information about including special characters, such as carriage returns, tabs, and quotes themselves.

Sample

You are writing a shell script and you want to display a message
on-screen. In the shell script, you include this line:

    echo "Your report is now printing!"

When you run the shell script, this line displays

    Your report is now printing!

ed

Runs one of the world's ugliest line-oriented text editors. Part IV
explains how to use it or preferably how to use a better text
editor, such as vi or emacs.

See also the section "Talk to Mr. ed" in Chapter 12 of *UNIX For
Dummies*.

elm

Lets you read and send mail. Part V explains how to use it.

See also the section "Playing Postman Pat with elm" in Chapter 18 of *UNIX For Dummies*.

emacs

Runs a powerful screen-oriented text editor. Part IV explains how to use it.

See also the section "A novel concept in editing: emacs makes sense" in Chapter 12 of *UNIX For Dummies*.

env

Shows you information about your UNIX environment variables.

UNIXspeak

env

Sample

You are wondering which environment variables are defined for you anyway. You type

```
env
```

You see a bunch of lines that look like this:

```
HOME=/usr/margy
TZ=AST4ADT
```

More stuff

On some BSD systems, this command is called printenv. *See also* set and setenv.

ex

A yucky line-oriented text editor that uses commands which are similar to ed and vi. It's an extended version of ed (hence the name). For maximum confusion, you can also use ex commands within vi. Part IV explains how to use them all.

See the section "Oh, no! It's my ex!" in Chapter 12 of *UNIX For Dummies*.

exit

Logs you out. When you use it in a terminal window, it closes the window.

UNIXspeak

    exit

Sample

You are finished working with UNIX and you want to go home. You type

    exit

You see a message saying that you have logged out.

Or you are using a terminal window in Motif and you are finished with it. To make it go away, you type

    exit

The window closes.

More stuff

If exit doesn't work, try typing logout. Pressing Ctrl-D may also log you out.

When you use Motif, typing exit in the log-in window (the first window created when Motif starts up) not only closes the window but also usually logs you out.

See the sections "Ciao, UNIX!" in Chapter 1 and "Getting Rid of Windows" in Chapter 11 of *UNIX For Dummies*.

fg

Continues a stopped job by running it in the foreground. (Some versions of the Bourne and Korn shells cannot do this.)

UNIXspeak

fg [%*job*]

Option or Argument	Function
%*job*	Specifies the job number you want to run in the foreground. If you leave it out, UNIX assumes that you mean the current job.

Sample

You are running a long, time-consuming program in the background by using the `bg` command (described earlier in this part of the book). You find out that you need the results in time for a big meeting in half an hour, so you decide to move it to the foreground. This means that you can't do any other work with your computer while the program runs, but it finishes as soon as possible.

To check that it's still running in the background, you type

```
jobs
```

You see your job listed as job number 2. You type

```
fg %2
```

Because the program runs in the foreground, you can't get any other work done, but it's running full-speed.

More stuff

Rather than use the job number from the `jobs` listing, you can use the first few letters of the program that is running. If the `find` program is running in the background, for example, you can move it to the foreground by typing

```
fg %find
```

See the section "The Magic of Job Control" in Chapter 15 of *UNIX For Dummies*.

file

Tells you whether something is a file, a directory, or something else entirely. If the thing is a file, the file command tries to guess which type of information it contains.

UNIXspeak

file *names*

Option or Argument	Function
names	Specifies the directories or files you want information about

Sample

You see an object named Updates in your home directory, and you wonder which it is. You type

    file Updates

You see something like this:

    Update: directory

You wonder what's in the directory, so you type

    file Updates/*

You see a list of the filenames in the directory, with a guess about each file's contents.

More stuff

The file command can determine whether a file contains ASCII text. If it does, it can recognize certain types of ASCII text files, such as those that contain nroff or troff commands. It also recognizes compressed files created by using the compress or pack programs. If file cannot tell what a file contains, it suggests that it is data. It uses some rules of thumb to guess what's in a file, so now and then it guesses wrong.

See nroff, troff, compress, and pack.

See the section "What's in That File?" in Chapter 13 of *UNIX For Dummies.*

find

Finds one or more files, assuming that you know their approximate filenames, and does something to them.

UNIXspeak

find *directories* [-name *filename*] [-user *username*]
[-atime +*days*] [-mtime +*days*] [-print] [-exec
command { } \;] [-ok *command* { } \;]

Option or Argument	Function
directories	Specifies a list of directories in which you want to begin the search. The find command searches all the subdirectories of these directories too. If you want to start in the current directory, just type a single period (.).
-name *filename*	Specifies the name of the file (or files) you want to find. If you don't know the exact name, you can use the wildcard characters ? and *. A ? stands for any single character, and a * stands for a group of characters. You must quote the filename if you use any wildcards.
-user *username*	Specifies the user who owns the files you want to find.
-atime +*days*	Specifies that you want only files which haven't been accessed (looked at) in at least *days* (the number of days). If you use a minus sign rather than the plus sign before the number of days, you get only files that were last looked at within that number of days.
-mtime +*days*	Specifies that you want only files which haven't been modified in at least *days* days. If you use a minus sign rather than the plus sign before the number of days, you get only files that were last changed within that number of days.

Option or Argument	Function
-print	Displays the names of files it finds. If you don't include this option, the `find` command may find lots of files, but it doesn't tell you about them.
-exec *command* {} \;	Runs the *command* every time it finds a file. When it runs the command, it substitutes the name of the file it found for the {}. Be sure to type \; at the end of the command.
-ok *command* {} \;	Works the same way as the `-exec` option, except that it asks you to confirm that you want to perform the command as it finds each file.

Sample

You know that you made a file called business.plan, but you cannot find it. Perhaps it's in the wrong subdirectory. In your home directory, you type

```
find . -name business.plan -print
```

UNIX tells you that a file by that name is in your Planning directory, like this:

```
./Planning/business.plan
```

Or you want to print all files with filenames that begin with *recipe*. You type

```
find -name "recipe*" -exec lpr {} \;
```

As UNIX finds each file, it runs the `lpr` command to print it and substitutes the filename for the {} on the command line. Notice that you must enclose the filename in quotation marks if it contains wildcard characters.

What if you are asked to delete some files because your department is running out of disk space? You decide to see whether you have files you haven't looked at in at least three months (90 days). You type

```
find -atime +90 -print
```

Alternatively, you want to see which files you have changed within the last week. You type

```
find -mtime -7 -print
```

More stuff

If you want to look in several places for a file, you can type several directories on the command line, like this:

```
find . /usr/john -name chapter3 -print
```

This command looks in the current working directory (and all its subdirectories) as well as in /usr/john (and all its subdirectories) for the file chapter3.

To search for a directory, use the -type d option, like this:

```
find . -name OldVersions -type d -print
```

This command searches for a directory named OldVersions.

To search for all the files you own (assuming that your username is harold), you type

```
find / -user harold -print
```

This command begins the search at the root directory (/) of the entire file system, so it might take a while.

See the sections "When You Care Enough to Know the Filename" in Chapter 26 and "The find Command" in Chapter 29 of *UNIX For Dummies*.

---

finger

Lists the people using your computer, with their real names, not just their UNIX usernames.

UNIXspeak

finger [*usernames*]

Option or Argument	Function
usernames	Specifies the user (or users) about whom you want more information

Sample

You are wondering who else is using your computer. You type

```
finger
```

You see a listing of usernames, real names, and other miscellaneous information. You notice a username you don't recognize, so you want more information. You type

`finger dougm`

You see several lines about your friend Doug Muder, including his full name, his home directory, which shell he runs, when he logged in, which project he's working on (assuming that this information is stored in a file named `.project`) in his home directory, and his plans (from a file named `.plan` in his home directory).

More stuff

You can also find out who is using other computers on your network. To find out who's on the `xuxa` system, you type

`finger @xuxa`

The @ tells UNIX that this is the name of a system, not the name of a user. To find out more about a user on another system, you type

`finger jordan@xuxa`

If you are on the Internet, you can get information about any user on any system on the entire network. To find out who is on an Internet system named `mit.edu`, for example, you type

`finger @mit.edu`

Some Internet systems respond with general information about the system rather than a list of who's logged on.

See also `who`.

 See the sections "Finding Out Who's on Your Computer" and "Finding Out Who's on Other Computers" in Chapter 17 of *UNIX For Dummies*.

ftp

 A file-transfer program, from one computer to another over a network. See Part VI for details.

grep

Finds lines in one or more files that contain a particular word or phrase.

UNIXspeak

grep [-i] [-l] [-v] *text filenames*

Option or Argument	Function
-i	Ignores case (uppercase and lowercase) when you're searching
-l	Displays only the names of the files that contain the text, not the actual lines
-v	Specifies that you are looking for lines that *don't* contain the *text*
text	Specifies the word or phrase to search for; if the text includes spaces or punctuation that might confuse UNIX, enclose it in quotation marks
filenames	Specifies the file (or files) in which to search; to search all the files in the current directory, type *

Sample

You are looking for the memo you wrote in which you mentioned "microwaveable shelf stable foods." To search all the files in the current directory, you type

```
grep "microwaveable shelf stable" *
```

You don't find the file you want. You realize that the M might be capitalized, so you tell grep to ignore capitalization by typing

```
grep -i "microwaveable shelf stable" *
```

More stuff

In addition to searching for just plain text, grep can search for all kinds of patterns. In fact, grep stands for *g*lobal *r*egular *e*xpression and *p*rint, and it searches for *regular expressions*. Luckily, regular expressions look just like text except for some punctuation that has special meanings to grep. The characters to watch out for are shown in the following table:

Character	Meaning
.	Matches any single character.
*	Matches any number of the character that precedes it. For example, .* means to match any number of any character. X* means any number of Xs.
[ ]	Matches any one of the characters inside the brackets. For example, [ABC] matches one A, one B, or one C. [A-Z] matches any capital letter.
^	Represents the beginning of the line. For example, ^T matches a T at the beginning of a line.
$	Represents the end of the line. For example, !$ matches an exclamation point at the end of a line.
\	Tells grep to take the next character literally, not as a special character. If you want to search for I.B.M., for example, you can type I\.B\.M\.

Related programs are egrep and fgrep. egrep is more powerful but more confusing, and fgrep is faster but more limited. For your sanity's sake, stick with grep.

See the sections "When You Don't Know the Filename" in Chapter 26 and "The grep Command" in Chapter 29 of *UNIX For Dummies*.

head

Displays just the first few lines of a file (usually the first ten).

UNIXspeak

head [*-lines*] *filename*

Option or Argument	Function
-lines	Specifies the number of lines you want to see; if you omit this option, you get ten lines
filename	Specifies the file you want to look at

Sample

You are wondering what's in a file, but because it's very large, you want to see just the beginning. You type

```
head master.plan
```

You see the first ten lines of the file.

More stuff

You decide that you want to see more. To see the fist 20 lines, you type

```
head -20 master.plan
```

To see the file one screen at a time, type

```
more master.plan
```

You can also use `head` to see the first few lines of the output of another command. To see just the first 15 lines of the `man` page about the `ls` command, you type

```
man ls | head -15
```

On systems without a `head` command, you can get the same effect with the `sed` command. `sed` does all kinds of things (described later in this part of the book), but its `q` option displays lines at the beginning of a file. You can display the first 20 lines of the `master.plan` file, for example, like this:

```
sed 20q master.plan
```

See the section "Looking at the Guts of a File" in Chapter 4 of *UNIX For Dummies*.

help

If your UNIX system has an on-line help system, displays possibly helpful information about commands.

UNIXspeak

```
help
```

Sample

On some UNIX systems, you can type

```
help
```

You see a little menu of topics, and you can display information about many UNIX commands.

Most UNIX systems, however, have no help system, and you see just an error message. It's worth a try, though.

See man to learn how to use the on-line reference manual.

history

Lists the last 20 or so commands you typed. Works with only the C and Korn shells.

UNIXspeak

history

Sample

You finally got a long, involved command to work (such as grep or find). A few minutes later, it has disappeared from the top of your screen (or terminal window). You want to give the command again. You type

history

You see a list of the last 20 or so commands, including the one you want to give again.

More stuff

If you use the C shell, you don't have to type the command again. Instead, you can reexecute the last command you gave by typing

!!

If the command you want is several commands back, you can still rerun it. To execute command number 5 in the history list, you type

!5

If the command you want is the most recent command you gave that begins with *gr,* you can type

!gr

If you use the Korn shell, you can also reexecute commands. To execute the last command again, you type

r

To rerun the last `grep` command, you type

```
r grep
```

If you use the Bourne shell, you are out of luck.

id

Tells you what your numeric user and group ID are and, on BSD, which groups you are in.

UNIXspeak

`id`

Sample

You want to know your user and group IDs so that you can tell your wizard what they are when you ask for help. You type

```
id
```

UNIX responds this way:

```
uid=275(johnl), group=50(staff)
```

See the section "Mother, May I?" in Chapter 28 of *UNIX For Dummies.*

jobs

Lists the jobs that are running in either the foreground or background or that are stopped. (Some versions of the Bourne and Korn shells cannot do this.)

UNIXspeak

`jobs`

Sample

Earlier in the day, you started a long, time-consuming job. You wonder whether it is still running, so you type

```
jobs
```

You see a list of all the jobs you are running, in either the foreground or the background, as well as any stopped jobs. (You can
stop the job in the foreground by pressing Ctrl-Z.)

More stuff

After you have listed your jobs, you can move jobs to the
foreground or the background — see bg and fg. For a general
description of job control, see the section "The Magic of Job
Control" in Chapter 15 of *UNIX For Dummies*.

kill

Cancels a job you don't want to continue.

UNIX*speak*

kill *%job*

or

kill [-9] *pid*

Option or Argument	Function
job	Specifies the job you want to kill. You can use the job number listed by the jobs command or the first few letters of the program that is running (C and Korn shells only).
-9	Tells kill to show no mercy in killing the program; kill it no matter what.
pid	Specifies the process ID of the job. You can use the ps command to find out the job's process ID. (See ps later in this part of the book.)

Sample

You begin running a program called big.report and you realize
that you did something wrong. You stop the job by pressing Ctrl-Z;
the message Stopped is displayed. To kill the program, you type

```
kill %bi
```

Because big.report is the only program you are running that begins with the letters *bi,* it dies.

More stuff

If a program is truly out of control, Ctrl-Z may not stop it. In this case, you may have to find out its process ID (*pid*) to kill it. Use the ps command to see its pid (5246, for example) and then type

```
kill -9 5246
```

You can cancel only your own jobs, not jobs run by that ape in the next cubicle.

For a description of how to kill programs that do not want to die, see the sections "The Magic of Job Control" in Chapter 15 and "Murder on the Process Express" in Chapter 23 of *UNIX For Dummies.*

---

ksh

Runs the Korn shell.

UNIXspeak

ksh [script]

Sample

A friend gives you a shell script named fix.it.up that you want to run. She tells you that the script works with the Korn shell, so you run it by typing

```
ksh fix.it.up
```

More stuff

When you use UNIX, you are always using a shell. The other shells are the Bourne shell (sh) and the C shell (csh). The ksh command is most often useful to run a Korn shell script that someone has given you.

For a description of UNIX shells, see the section "Cracking the Shell" in Chapter 2 of *UNIX For Dummies.*

ln

Creates a new link to a file. Additional links can give a file more than one name or can make it live in more than one directory.

UNIXspeak

`ln` [-n] [-s] ***existingfile newname***

or

`ln` [-n] [-s] ***existingfiles directory***

Option or Argument	Function
-n	Tells `ln` not to clobber existing files when you're creating new links (a good idea)
-s	Tells `ln` to make a symbolic link to the file (not on older System V systems)
existingfile	Specifies the file to which you want to create a new link
newname	Specifies the name to give to the new link
existingfiles	Specifies the file (or files) to which you want to create a new link (or links)
directory	Specifies the directory in which you want the new link (or links)

Sample

You and your friend Katy both play backgammon, and she has a great new public-domain backgammon game in the `bin` sub-directory of her home directory. Rather than make a copy of the program, which would waste space on the disk, you create a link to the file in Katy's directory. You move to your `bin` directory and type

```
ln /usr/katy/bin/backgammon backg
```

Now the filename `backg` also appears in your `bin` directory, and it refers to the same file as `/usr/katy/bin/backgammon`. If you want to create a link in the current directory using the file's original name, you could have typed

```
ln /usr/katy/bin/backgammon .
```

What if you want to create links to all the files in Katy's directory? You type (including the period)

```
ln /usr/katy/bin/* .
```

More stuff

A link to a file created by using the `ln` command works exactly the same way as the original filename for the file. You can use the `mv` command to rename the link, the `cp` command to copy the file, and the `rm` command to remove the link. (When you remove a link, the file may still remain. A file is deleted when its last link is removed.)

If you use files on other computers by way of NFS or some other system, you cannot create regular links to those files — you see a message saying `ln: different file system`. Instead, you can create *soft links* by using the `-s` option with the `ln` command.

If a file (or a link) already has the same name as the link you are creating, some versions of `ln` destroy the exiting file (or link) and create the new one. It's a good idea to use the `ls` command beforehand, to check whether a file already has the name you plan to use. Then use the `-n` option of the `ln` command so that it asks before clobbering existing files.

See the sections "When You Want To Share a File" in Chapter 26 and "The `ln` command" in Chapter 29 of *UNIX For Dummies*.

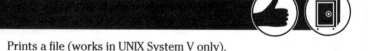

lp

Prints a file (works in UNIX System V only).

UNIXspeak

```
lp [-c] [-d printer] [-m] [-n copies]
[-o options] [-P pagenumbers] [-w] filename
```

Option or Argument	Function
-c	Tells `lp` to make a copy of the file to be printed; if you edit the file between the time you give the `lp` command and when it is printed, the changes don't appear in the printout

Option or Argument	Function
-d *printer*	Specifies the printer on which you want the file printed
-m	Tells lp to send you e-mail when the file has been printed; useful when the printer is very busy and you may have to wait your turn
-n *copies*	Specifies the number of copies of the file to print
-o *options*	Specifies print options, listed later in this section
-P *pagenumbers*	Specifies which pages to print (that's a capital *P*)
-w	Displays a message on your screen as soon as the file has printed
filename	Specifies the file you want to print

Sample

You have just created a text file that contains some important financial information you want to pass along to your boss. You type

```
lp fin.info
```

After you print it, you decide that you want two more copies, so you type

```
lp -n 2 fin.info
```

More stuff

In response to the lp command, you see a message like this:

```
request id is lj-1024 (1 file)
```

The request ID number can be useful if you decide to cancel printing the file (see cancel earlier in this part of the book).

Suppose that you want to print your file on the high-quality printer in the executive suite, on a printer named execlaser. You type

```
lp -d execlaser fin.info
```

If many people share one printer, a long delay can occur before your file is printed. If you want to see a message on-screen when the file prints, you can type

```
lp -w fin.info
```

Or `lp` can send you electronic mail when the file has been printed, if you type

```
lp -m fin.info
```

If you want to print the output of another command, use redirection. To print a directory of files, for example, you can type

```
ls | lp
```

If you want to print several files, you can type several filenames, like this:

```
lp fin.info memo4 letter.to.mom
```

Depending on the capabilities of your printer, you may be able to control the format of the output with the options in the following table, which you type right after the `-o` option:

Option	*Description*
nobanner	Doesn't print a banner page (a page with your username and the name of the file). UNIX usually prints a banner page before each print job, to separate one from the next.
nofilebreak	Doesn't start each file on a new page.
cpi=*pitch*	Prints the file at *pitch* characters per inch. Your printer may be capable of printing at a limited number of pitches, usually only 10 or 12.
lpi=*lines*	Prints the file at *lines* lines per inch (usually six). Some printers can print eight lines per inch.
length=*inches*i	Prints pages that are *inches* inches long (be sure to include the small *i* at the end of the option).
length=*lines*l	Prints pages that are *lines* lines long (be sure to include the small *l*).
width=*chars*	Prints a maximum of *chars* characters per line.
width=*inches*i	Prints pages that are a maximum of *inches* inches wide.

To print several files with no page breaks between them, for example, you can type

```
lp -o nofilebreak fin*
```

See the sections "Printing Stuff" in Chapter 9 and "The lp
Command (UNIX System V Only)" in Chapter 29 of *UNIX For
Dummies.*

lpq

Lists the status of all the available printers (works in BSD UNIX
only).

UNIXspeak

lpq [-a] [*printer*]

Option or Argument	Function
-a	Lists information about all printers
printer	Specifies the printer you want to know about; if you don't specify the printer, it assumes a default, usually the printer closest to you

Sample

You have tried to print several large documents, but they haven't
appeared on the printer. To look at the print queue for your
printer, which is named *laser*, you type

    lpq laser

UNIX responds

    no entries

Hmm . . . nothing there. Maybe the documents are waiting to print
on some other printer. To see the print queues for all the available printers, you type

    lpq -a

See the sections "Cancel the order, BSD" in Chapter 9 and "The
lpq Command (BSD UNIX only)" in Chapter 29 of *UNIX For
Dummies.*

lpr

Prints a file (works in BSD UNIX only).

UNIXspeak

lpr [-Pprinter] filename

Option or Argument	Function
-Pprinter	Specifies which printer to use
filename	Specifies the file you want to print

Sample

You have received a terrific-looking recipe for Brazilian black beans, in a text file named feijoada. To print it, you type

    lpr feijoada

If you decide to print it on a printer named hplj, you type

    lpr -Phplj feijoada

More stuff

You can also print the output of another command. For example, this line shows how to print a man page:

    man chmod | lpr

See the sections "Printing Stuff" in Chapter 9 and "The lpr Command (BSD UNIX only)" in Chapter 29 of *UNIX For Dummies*.

lpstat

Lists the status of all available printers (works in UNIX System V only).

UNIXspeak

lpstat [-a all] [-d] [-p *printers*]

Option or Argument	Function
-a all	Lists all printers that are available
-d	Lists your default printer (the printer on which your files print unless you specify otherwise)
-p *printers*	Displays the status of the printer (or printers) you name

Sample

You have sent a large document to be printed, but you change your mind. To find out its request ID, you type

    lpstat

You see a list of the print jobs waiting to be printed on your printer, including the request ID of each one. To cancel the job with request ID hplj-78344, you type

    cancel hplj-78344

More stuff

You are wondering which printers are out there on your network. You type

    lpstat -a all

You see a list of printers, one per line, with the name and status of each one. If the printer is accepting requests, you can use it. To find out whether several print jobs are in the print queue for a particular printer (one named execlaser, for example), you type

    lpstat -p execlaser

 See the sections "Cancel the order, System V" in Chapter 9 and "The lpstat Command (UNIX System V Only)" in Chapter 29 of *UNIX For Dummies*.

 ls

Lists the files in a directory.

UNIXspeak

    ls [-a] [-l] [-p] [-r] [-R] [-t] [-x]
    [pathnames]

Option or Argument	Function
-a	Displays all the files and subdirectories, including hidden files (with names that begin with a dot)
-l	Displays detailed information about each file and directory, including permissions, owners, size, and when the file was last modified
-p	Display a slash (/) at the end of each directory name, to distinguish them from filenames
-r	Display files in reverse order
-R	Include the contents of all subdirectories too
-t	Display files in order of modification time
-x	Display the filenames in several columns across the screen
pathnames	File or directory to list

Sample

You are working in your home directory and you want to see a list of the files in it. You type

```
ls
```

But what about your hidden files, such as .login and .profile? To see information about all your files, you type

```
ls -a
```

More stuff

If you want to see the sizes and modification dates of all your files, you can type

```
ls -al
```

(You can combine several options together after one dash, to save typing.) This "long format" listing looks like this:

```
-rwxr-xr-x 2 mgmt john 14675 Nov 9 15:34 fin.info
-rw-rw-rw- 1 mgmt margy 3827 Nov 6 19:43 baked.beans
drw-rw-rw- 16 mgmt margy 128 Oct 1 11:31 Mail
```

This listing contains the following eight columns:

Column	Description
Permissions	The first letter indicates whether it is a file (-) or a directory (d). The remaining nine characters are in groups of three: the first group shows the owner's permissions, the second group shows the group's permissions, and the third group shows everyone else's permissions. Each group of three characters includes the read (r or -), write (w or -), and execute (x or -) permission. A dash indicates that the permission isn't granted. The permissions -rwxr-xr-, for example, indicate that it is a file (not a directory); its owner can read, write, and execute it; its group can read or execute it but not write on it; and everyone else can read it but not write or execute it.
Links	The number of names (links) the file has. For directories, this is the number of files in the directory plus 2.
Group owner	The name of the group that owns this file.
User owner	The name of the user who owns this file.
Size	The size of the file in bytes (characters).
Mod. date	The date on which the file was last modified.
Mod. time	The time when the file was last modified.
Filename	The name of the file.

Suppose that the directory listing shows that you have a subdirectory named bin (the bin directory usually contains programs you use). To see what it contains, you type

```
ls -l bin
```

Suppose that you are looking for a filename which begins with bud. You hope that it is in your home directory or a subdirectory of it. You type

```
ls -R bud*
```

To list all the information about your files, sorted in reverse order of modification time, you type

```
ls -ltr
```

If a directory listing is too long to fit on-screen, redirect its output to the more command so that you can see one page at a time, like this:

```
ls -al q* | more
```

Alternatively, you list the filenames across the screen, by typing this line:

```
ls -x
```

The ls command has about 14 trillion options, and no one knows them all. If you want to flummox a self-appointed UNIX expert, ask which lowercase letters are *not* valid options to ls.

See the sections "What Files Do You Have?" in Chapter 4 and "The ls Command" in Chapter 29 of *UNIX For Dummies*.

---

mail

Lets you read and send mail. See Part V to learn how to use it.

See also the section "Playing Postman Pat with mail" in Chapter 18 of *UNIX For Dummies*.

---

man

Displays reference manual page about a UNIX command.

UNIXspeak

man [-] [-k *keywords*] **topic**

Option or Argument	Function
-	If your UNIX system usually presents manual pages one screen at a time, this option displays them without stopping, which is useful in redirecting the output of man to a file or to the printer.

Option or Argument	Function
-k *keywords*	Specifies one or more keywords to search for. You see all man pages that contain the keyword (or keywords) in their header lines.
topic	Specifies the topic about which you want information. Available man pages include primarily UNIX commands, with a small number of general topics.

Sample

You have forgotten the multitude of options you can use with the ls command, so you type

    man ls

On some systems, the manual pages scroll right off the top of your screen (other UNIX systems automatically use more with man so that you see one screen at a time). You type

    man ls | more

To save this information for later perusal or inclusion in a user's manual you are writing for your department, you type

    man ls > ls.info

More stuff

To print a manual page, you can type

    man ls | lp

(If you use BSD UNIX, redirect output to lpr instead.)

If you use Motif or another X Windows system, trying running xman rather than man.

For details about how to read a manual page, see the section "Ten Times More Information Than You Want about UNIX" in Chapter 27 of *UNIX For Dummies*.

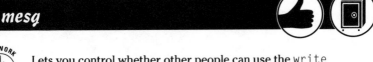

mesg

Lets you control whether other people can use the write command to interrupt you with on-screen messages.

UNIXspeak

mesg [n|y]

Option or Argument	Function
n	Prevents messages from other users from popping up on your screen
y	Allows messages to appear on your screen

Sample

Dave down the hall, who always did have a weird sense of humor, insists on using the write command (described later in this part of the book) to send cute messages to you every five or ten minutes. The messages distract you and mess up your screen. Despite your pleading, he doesn't stop. In retaliation, you type

```
mesg n
```

Now if Dave tries to send a message, he sees

```
Permission denied.
```

More stuff

If your pals like to interrupt you with write messages, tell them to send you electronic mail instead. The nice thing about e-mail is that you can read it when you want to.

mkdir

Creates a new directory.

UNIXspeak

mkdir *directory*

Option or Argument	Function
directory	Specifies the name of the new directory. If the name doesn't begin with a slash, the new directory is created as a subdirectory of the current working directory. If the name begins with a slash, the name defines the path from the root directory to the new directory.

Sample

You want a place to store some files temporarily. In your home directory, you type

```
mkdir Temp
```

The next time you use the `ls` command, the `Temp` directory appears in your home directory.

More stuff

You must have permission to write in a directory to create a subdirectory in it. For the most part, you should create directories in your own home directories or subdirectories of it.

See the sections "Making directories" in Chapter 5 and "The `mkdir` Command" in Chapter 29 of *UNIX For Dummies*.

---

more

Displays information one screen at a time so that you have time to read it.

UNIX*speak*

more [-1] [-r] [-s] [-u] [+*linenum*] [+/*text*]
[*filename*]

Option or Argument	Function
-l	Ignores form-feed characters in the file (Ctrl-L, which starts a new page). Use this option if the file has a large number of tiny pages of text.
-r	Displays control characters instead of performing their function. For example, the control character Ctrl-H is a backspace: Rather than backspace, this option displays Ctrl-H as ^H.
-s	Squeezes out extra blank lines by displaying only one blank line.
-u	Ignores underscore and backspace characters, which can otherwise make text unreadable on-screen.
+*linenum*	Displays the file (or whatever the input to more is) as line *linenum*.
+/*text*	Begins displaying text two lines before the first time *text* appears.
filename	Specifies the file to display.

Sample

You have received a long memo in a text file. To display it on your screen, you type

```
more long.memo
```

After displaying one screen of text, more pauses. Type a space to see the next screen of text.

More stuff

When more pauses at the end of a screen, you can press any of the following keys:

Key	Meaning
Space	Displays the next screen of text
Enter or Return	Displays the next line of text
h	Displays help about what these keys mean
q	Quits displaying this file

Key	Meaning
/	Searches for some text. Type the text to search for immediately after the /, followed by Enter or Return

The more command is frequently used with redirection, to display the output of another command. To see a long directory listing one screen at a time, for example, you type

```
ls | more
```

See the sections "Gimme just a little at a time" in Chapter 6 and "The more Command" in Chapter 29 of *UNIX For Dummies*.

mv

Renames a file or moves it from one directory to another.

UNIXspeak

mv [-i] *oldname newname*

or

mv [-i] *filename directory*[/*newname*]

Option or Argument	Function
-i	Tells mv to inquire before clobbering an existing file with a moved or renamed file (works only in UNIX System V Release 4)
oldname	Specifies the existing file you want to rename
newname	Specifies the new name to use for the file
filename	Specifies the file you want to move
directory	Specifies the directory into which you want to move the file

Sample

A co-worker gives you a file named old.budget. You want to give it a better name, so you type

```
mv old.budget 1993.budget
```

Then you decide to move it into your Budget directory. You type

    mv 1993.budget Budget

More stuff

You can move and rename a file at the same time. If you want to move your new.recipe file into your Recipes directory, for example, and rename it at the same time, you can type

    mv new.recipe Recipes/veg.lasagne

You can also rename and move entire directories. Suppose that you want to rename your Recipes directory. You type

    mv Recipes Food

The directory gets a new name. This operation doesn't affect the files in the directory.

Or suppose that you want to move your Recipes directory to be a subdirectory of your Personal directory. You type

    mv Recipes Personal

If a file already has the name you want to use, mv deletes it without telling you and replaces it with the renamed or moved file. To avoid this situation, use the -i option (for UNIX System V Release 4 users only). Or use the ls command first to make sure that no file in the directory has the name you want to use.

See the sections "What's in a Name (Reprise)" in Chapter 4, "Transplanting files" and "Renaming a directory" in Chapter 5, and "The mv Command" in Chapter 29 of *UNIX For Dummies. See also* the sidebar "Links, copies, moves, truncation, and other details about file destruction" in Chapter 22 to see how mv works with files that have more than one name (link).

---

nice

Runs a command with lower priority so that it doesn't hog the computer.

UNIXspeak

nice *command* [*arguments*] [*&*]

Option or Argument	Function
command	Specifies the command you want to run
arguments	If you want to provide arguments for the command, type them just as you would if you weren't using the nice command
&	Runs the command in the background; no one ever uses nice to run programs in the foreground

Sample

You usually run your monthly invoice report by typing

```
invoice.rpt 1994.12
```

except that you use different filenames for the argument: 1994.12 contains the data for one month.

The program slows the computer down like crazy, however, and your co-workers complain. So you decide to run it in the background with low priority so that it takes longer but doesn't slow the system down so much. You type

```
nice invoice.rpt 1994.12 &
```

You see the process ID (pid) of the job and another prompt, so you can do other work in the foreground while your program runs in the background.

More stuff

Many shells automatically nice anything that was begun with &, so you may not have to.

 See the section "Starting Background Processes" in Chapter 15 of *UNIX For Dummies*.

pack

Shrinks a file into one "packed" file so that it takes up less space on your disk.

UNIXspeak

```
pack filenames
```

Option or Argument	Function
filenames	Specifies the files to compress

Sample

You have finished writing a large report and you want to save it in a compressed format to save space. You type

```
pack long.report
```

pack makes a packed file named long.report.z that contains a shrunken version of the file and deletes the original file.

More stuff

When you want to get your files back from a packed file, you use unpack (described later in this part of the book).

It's a good idea to pack your files before transferring them over the network to another computer. The smaller the file, the faster it transfers.

See also compress, uncompress, and pcat. The compress command usually does a better job than pack does.

See the section "Squashing Your Files" in Chapter 13 of *UNIX For Dummies.*

---

passwd

Changes your password.

UNIXspeak

```
passwd [-s]
```

Option or Argument	Function
-s	Displays status information, including your username, whether you have a password, and when you last changed it. This option does *not* display your password, though! (Indeed, if you forget your password, there's no way to get it back, although the administrator can change it to something else for you.)

Sample

You fell asleep at the keyboard and you think that you may have talked in your sleep. Just in case you mumbled your password, you decide to change it. Besides, your current password is *sue* and you just read somewhere that this password is the most common password in the U.S. You type

```
passwd
```

It prompts you for your current password to prove that you really are you. Then it asks you to enter a new password twice. Because the password doesn't appear on-screen, typing it twice ensures that no typo occurred while you typed it (or that the same typo occurred both times).

More stuff

You have to know your password to be able to change it. This requirement prevents a passerby from changing your password while you are off getting coffee. If you forget your password, ask your system administrator (nicely!) to give you a new one. Many versions of passwd try to enforce such rules as the password must be at least seven characters, contain digits, and otherwise be hard to remember. Often if you try an unacceptable password three or four times, passwd gives up and accepts it.

See the section "Password Smarts" in Chapter 1 of *UNIX For Dummies.*

pr

Formats a text file with page numbers, line numbers, or other options so that it looks nice when you print it.

UNIXspeak

```
pr [-a] [-d] [-f] [-F] [-h text] [-l lines]
[-m] [-n] [-o offset] [-t] [-w width]
[+pagenum] [-columns] filenames
```

Option or Argument	Function
-a	Prints lines across the page. This option is great when you have lots of short lines.
-d	Double-spaces the output.
-f	Uses form-feed characters rather than blank lines to move to the top of a new page.
-F	Wraps long lines around to the beginning of the next line rather than cut them off. (Stands for *f*old.)
-h *text*	Prints *text* as the header at the top of each page. If you omit this option, pr prints a header that consists of the filename and the date the file was last changed.
-l *lines*	Sets the page length to *lines* lines. If you omit this option, the page length is 66 lines, which is correct when you're printing at six lines per inch on 11-inch paper.
-m	Merges several files together and prints each one in a separate column.
-n	Numbers the lines of the file.
-o *offset*	Prints *offset* extra spaces at the beginning of each line, to make a wider left margin. This option is useful if you plan to punch holes in the paper or bind it.
-t	Suppresses printing of page headers or blank lines at the end of a file.
-w *width*	Sets the line width to *width* characters. If you leave this option out, the line width is 72 characters. Interesting only if you use multiple columns.
+*pagenum*	Begins printing at page *pagenum*.
-*columns*	Prints the file in multiple columns, as in a newspaper or magazine. *Columns* is the number of columns you want.
filenames	Specifies the file (or files) you want to format for printing.

Sample

You have written an interesting short story and want to print a nicely formatted draft. You type

```
pr choco.story | lp
```

This command formats the `choco.story` file and redirects the result to the `lp` command for printing. (If you use BSD UNIX, use the `lpr` command rather than `lp`.)

The last (fourth) page is smudged, so you reprint it by typing

```
pr +4 choco.story | lp
```

More stuff

Looking at the output, you decide to number the lines so that your short-story class can easily discuss it in detail and to print *My Life with Chocolate* as the heading on each page. You type

```
pr -n -h "My Life with Chocolate" choco.story | lp
```

Later, after you have translated the story into Portuguese, you want to print the original and the translation side-by-side. Also, you want to add a one-inch (10 character) left margin. You type

```
pr -o10 -m choco.story choco.story.port | lp
```

Notice that you can use `pr` only with text files, not with word processing documents, PostScript output files, or other data files.

See the section "Prettying Up Your Printouts" in Chapter 9 of *UNIX For Dummies*.

ps

Displays information about your processes (jobs).

UNIXspeak (BSD UNIX)

ps [-a] [-l] [-t*tty*] [-u] [-x]

Option or Argument	Function
-a	Displays information about all processes; if you omit this option, you see only your processes
-l	Displays a longer, more detailed version
-t*tty*	Displays a list of processes that were started by terminal *tty*
-u	Displays a "user-oriented" report with additional information
-x	Displays all processes that are running in the background and not using a terminal

UNIXspeak (UNIX System V)

ps [-a] [-e] [-f] [-t *ttys*] [-u *usernames*]

Option or Argument	Function
-a	Includes information about almost all processes, not just processes you started
-e	Displays all the processes in the entire system
-f	Displays a "full," more detailed listing
-t*ttys*	Displays a list of processes that were started by terminal (or terminals) *ttys*
-u*usernames*	Displays a list of processes that were started by the specified username (or usernames)

Sample (BSD UNIX)

You are wondering whether the process you ran in the background is still running or what. You type

```
ps
```

to see a list of all your processes. To see more information about them, you type

```
ps -l
```

No option lets you see processes started by a particular user. Instead, you can use grep to find them. To see all the processes that were started by lee, you type

```
ps -aux | grep lee
```

Sample (UNIX System V)

You think that a program might be running amok, so you type

```
ps
```

to see a list of all your processes. To see more information about them, you type

```
ps -f
```

You want to check on your friend Lee's processes too, so you type

```
ps -u lee
```

More stuff

The ps command produces a listing with one process per line. The columns you see depend on whether you use BSD UNIX or UNIX System V and which options you use.

Column	Description
PID	Process ID, the unique number assigned to the process. You use the PID to kill the process if it gets out of control (see kill earlier in this part of the book).
TTY or TT	Terminal ID where the process was run.
TIME	The number of minutes and seconds the process has run, counting only the time during which the process had the computer's full attention.
COMMAND	Command that began the process, more or less.
UID or USER	Username of the user who began the process.
PPID	PID of the process's *parent process* (the process that started this process). Sometimes, typing one command starts several processes.
C	Magic number related to how much CPU time the program has used lately.
STIME	Start time (the time of day when the process began). If it began more than 24 hours ago, this column shows the date.
STAT	Status of the process (R or 0 means that it is running right now).
%CPU	Percentage of the available central processing time the process has taken recently.
%MEM	Percentage of the available system memory the process has taken recently.
SZ	Total memory size of the program, measured in kilobytes.
RSS	How much memory the process is using right now, measured in kilobytes.

To find out how long you have been logged in, the number of people using your computer, and other fun facts, try typing uptime. You can also use the w command for information about users and processes.

See the section "Any Processes in the House?" in Chapter 23 of *UNIX For Dummies*.

pwd

Displays the name of the current working directory.

UNIXspeak

pwd

Sample

You are lost and want to know which directory you are in (what the current working directory is). So you type

    pwd

You see a pathname like this:

    /usr/margy/Recipes

See the sections "I've been working in the directory" in Chapter 5 and "The pwd Command" in Chapter 29 of *UNIX For Dummies*.

rcp

Copies files to or from another computer (it stands for *r*emote *c*opy). See Part VI for details.

rehash

Updates the table of UNIX commands and the programs they run (used only with the C shell).

UNIXspeak

rehash

Sample

You have just written a shell script, which is stored in a file named do.it in your bin directory. For UNIX to be capable of finding this new program when you type **do.it,** you update UNIX's command table by typing

    rehash

More stuff

If you don't run rehash, UNIX can find your new program only when it is in the current directory. After you run rehash, it can find the program no matter what the current directory is. The program must be stored in a directory that is included in your PATH environment variable.

See the section "Stuffing the bin" in Chapter 14 of *UNIX For Dummies*.

---

rlogin

Logs in to another computer (it stands for *remote login*). See Part VI for details.

---

rm

Deletes (removes) a file permanently.

UNIXspeak

rm [-i] [-r] *filenames*

Option or Argument	Function
-i	Asks you to confirm that you want to delete each file.
-r	Deletes an entire directory and all the files it contains. Watch out — you can do a great deal of damage with this option! Always use the -i option too.
filenames	Specifies the file (or files) to delete.

Sample

You made a test file and now you are finished with it. You type

    rm text.junk

It disappears from your directory.

Suppose that you want to delete all your old budget files. First, you make sure that you know what you are planning to delete, so you type

```
ls budget.93.*
```

If the list of files you see looks right, you delete them:

```
rm budget.93.*
```

More stuff

If other links (names) to the file exist, the file continues to exist. rm just deletes the name (link) you specify. A file actually dies when its last link (name) is deleted.

If you delete a file by mistake, talk to your system administrator immediately. A backup copy of the file may be on tape (or may not be, however).

See the sections "Nuking Files Back to the Stone Age" in Chapter 4, "How To Clobber Files" in Chapter 22, and "The rm Command" in Chapter 29 of *UNIX For Dummies*.

rmdir

Deletes (removes) a directory.

UNIXspeak

rmdir *directory*

Option or Argument	Function
directory	Specifies the directory you want to delete (it must be empty already)

Sample

Hooray! The budget process is over! After making backup copies of your files on a tape, you want to delete your Budget directory. First, you make sure that it doesn't contain anything you want to keep, so you type

```
ls Budget
```

All the files listed are files you want to delete, so you type

```
rm Budget/*
```

The Budget directory is now empty, so you type

```
rmdir Budget
```

More stuff

To delete a directory and all the files in it, you can use the rm -ir command (see rm earlier in this part of the book). You cannot delete the current working directory, so move to its parent (by typing **cd ..**) before deleting a directory.

See the sections "Amputating unnecessary directories" in Chapter 5 and "The rmdir Command" in Chapter 29 of *UNIX For Dummies*.

rn

Reads newsgroups (see Part VI).

rsh

Runs a command on another computer (it stands for *r*emote *sh*ell). See Part VI for details.

script

Saves in a text file the conversation you are having with UNIX (stores everything you type and everything UNIX types back at you). Works with BSD UNIX and UNIX System V Release 4 only.

UNIXspeak

```
script [-a filename]
```

Option or Argument	Function
-a *filename*	Specifies the file in which to store the information (if the file exists, it adds the new information to the end). If you don't use this option, script stores the text in a file named typescript.

Sample

You want to record your commands and UNIX's responses so that you can show your new trainee how to do something. Before giving the first command, you type

```
script
```

Then you give your usual series of commands. When you are finished, you type exit to leave script.

More stuff

If you are having trouble getting something done, this command can be a useful way to show a wizard what you did and what UNIX did to you.

sdiff

Compares two files by listing them side by side.

UNIXspeak

sdiff [-s] [-w *width*] *filename1 filename2*

Option or Argument	Function
-s	Suppresses printing of identical lines and prints only those that differ
-w *width*	Specifies the width of your screen (use -w 80)
filename1	Specifies one file to compare
filename2	Specifies the other file to compare

Sample

Your boss made some edits to your file. You want to know what they were, so you compare the edited version to your original by typing

```
sdiff memo4 memo4.original
```

5

More stuff

If the lines in the two files differ, UNIX puts a symbol in the column between the two files. If the line is in only the first file, the symbol is <; if it exists in only the second file, the symbol is >; and if the lines are different in the two files, the symbol is |.

See also cmp and diff.

sed

Lets you use prerecorded commands to make changes to text (it stands for *stream editor*).

UNIXspeak

sed [-f *commandfile*] [*commands*] **filenames**

Option or Argument	Function
-f *commandfile*	Specifies the file that contains the sed commands.
commands	Specifies sed commands to perform. If they contain spaces or punctuation, enclose them in quotes.
filenames	Specifies the file (or files) that contains the original text.

Sample

You want to look at the first 20 lines of a file. The q command quits when it gets to the specified line, so you type

```
sed 20q longfile
```

sed displays the file and quits after the 20th line. Or you can display the first 15 lines of output from the manual page about the ls command, like this:

```
man ls | sed 15q
```

Or you want to replace all instances of able with baker in a text file. You can use the s command, like this:

```
sed "s/Able/Baker/g" letter3 > letter3.new
```

This command reads the file letter3, changes Able to Baker wherever it occurs, and stores the result in letter3.new.

More stuff

If you want to create your own sed programs, read a good book about it, such as O'Reilly & Associates' *sed & awk,* by Dale Dougherty. The commands for sed are almost exactly the same as the ones for ed, described in Part IV.

---

set

Sets a shell variable to the value you specify or displays the value of the shell variable.

UNIXspeak (Bourne and Korn shells)

set

UNIXspeak (C shell)

set [*variable* = *value*]

Option or Argument	Function
variable	Specifies the variable whose value you want to set
value	Specifies the value you want to assign to the variable

Sample (Bourne and Korn shells)

You want to set a shell variable to the name of a directory you frequently use. You type the following line (no spaces allowed).

```
WORKDIR=/usr/fred/project/
```

Now you can use WORKDIR as the project directory name in your commands, like this:

```
cd $WORKDIR
```

In the Bourne and Korn shells, variable names are usually spelled with capital letters.

Sample (C shell)

You want to set a shell variable to the name of a directory you frequently use. You type

```
set workdir=/usr/fred/project/
```

Now you can use `workdir` as the project directory name in your commands, like this:

```
cd $workdir
```

In the C shell, variable names are usually spelled with small letters.

To set the value of an environment variable (a variable that is maintained by the shell and contains information about the shell environment), in the C shell you use the `setenv` command, described later in this part of the book. In the Bourne and Korn shells, you type `export WORKDIR` to make `WORKDIR` an environment variable.

More stuff (any shell)

To see a list of the defined variables in your shell, you type

```
set
```

To see the value of one variable, use the `echo` command like this:

```
echo $WORKDIR
```

UNIX forgets the variables you define when you log out. If you want to define a variable so that UNIX remembers it, include in your `.login` or `.profile` file the command that defines the variable.

To get rid of a variable right away rather than wait until the next time you log out, use the `unset` command.

setenv

Sets the value of an environment variable (C shell only).

UNIXspeak

setenv [*variable* [*value*]]

Option or Argument	Function
variable	Specifies the variable whose value you want to set.
value	Specifies the value you want to assign to the variable. If you leave it out, UNIX assigns nothing to the variable (the "null" value).

Sample

The PATH variable contains the list of directory pathnames that UNIX searches whenever you type the name of a program. All your frequently run programs should be stored in directories on the PATH list.

Suppose that you want to see your PATH list. You type

```
echo $PATH
```

Suppose that you have a bin subdirectory of your home directory and that it contains programs. You want to add this directory to your PATH list. You type

```
setenv PATH $PATH:/usr/margy/bin
```

This line sets the PATH variable to its current value, followed by the pathname /usr/margy/bin (substitute your username instead of margy).

More stuff

To see a list of your environment variables and their values, you type

```
setenv
```

Notice that there is no equal sign in the setenv command, even though you have to use one with the set command. It's darned confusing.

sh

Runs the Bourne shell.

UNIXspeak

sh [*scriptname*]

Option or Argument	Function
scriptname	Name of a file that contains a Bourne shell script

Sample

A friend gives you a shell script named check.all.files that you want to run. She tells you that the script works with the Bourne shell, so you run it by typing

```
sh check.all.files
```

More stuff

When you use UNIX, you are always using a shell. The other shells are the C shell (csh) and the Korn shell (ksh). You're likely to run sh yourself only to use it to run a shell script that someone has given you.

If you receive a *shar message* by way of electronic mail, you run it as a shell script to create a file. A shar message is a sneaky way to send nontext files (short programs and shell scripts) through the mail. To recover the file from a shar message, save the message as a text file (see Part V), use a text editor to remove all the lines from the beginning of the file to the first line that begins with a #, and then feed the file to the shell. If you save the shar message in a file called shar.msg, for example, you would type

```
sh shar.msg
```

This command runs the script in the shar file and creates the program files it contains. (At the beginning of most shar messages is a list of the files it creates.)

For a description of UNIX shells, see the section "Cracking the Shell" in Chapter 2 of *UNIX For Dummies;* for more information about shar messages, see the section "Sneaking Software Through the Mail" in Chapter 14.

sleep

Waits a little while, which is measured in seconds.

UNIXspeak

```
sleep time
```

Option or Argument	Function
time	Specifies the number of seconds to wait

Sample

In a shell script, you want to pause before performing a command. You include this line in the shell script:

```
sleep 5
```

When you run the script, it pauses for five seconds when it executes the sleep command.

More stuff

There's not much reason to use this command except in a shell script. If you want to execute a command at a particular time, see at and crontab.

See the section "Calendar Games" in Chapter 13 of *UNIX For Dummies*.

sort

Sorts the lines in a text file.

UNIXspeak

```
sort [-b] [-d] [-f] [-i] [-m] [-M] [-n] [-r]
[-u] [+fields] filename [-o outputfile]
```

Option or Argument	Function
-b	Ignores spaces at the beginning of the line.
-d	Uses dictionary sort order and ignores punctuation.
-f	Ignores capitalization while sorting.
-i	Ignores nonprinting control characters.
-m	Merges two or more input files into one sorted output.

Option or Argument	Function
-M	Treats the first three characters of each line as a three-letter month abbreviation and sorts by month order (Jan before Feb).
-n	Sorts based on the number at the beginning of the line. With this option, 99 precedes 100 rather than follows it, as it does in usual alphabetical order.
-r	Sorts in reverse order. You can combine this option with any other option.
-u	If the same line occurs in the file more than once, output it only once (stands for *u*nique).
+*fields*	Considers each line to contain a series of fields (fields are separated by tab characters). When you're sorting, *fields* specifies the number of fields to skip from the left end of the line. For example, sort +2 sorts beginning at the third field on each line.
filename	Specifies the file that contains the text to be sorted.
-o *outputfile*	Specifies that sort should send the sorted output to a file and specifies the name of the file.

Sample

You want to sort a list of names into alphabetical order. You type

```
sort name.list > sorted.list
```

The sorted text is stored in a new file named sorted.list.

More stuff

You can also sort the output of another command. For example, you can sort the list of lines that grep outputs, like this:

```
grep "eggplant parm" recipe.list | sort
```

The output of a number of commands (including `ls`) consists of fields separated by tabs, so you can sort it by using the +*fields* option. To sort a listing of files in numeric order by the fifth field (the file size), for example, you can type

```
ls -l | sort -n +5
```

See the sections "Sorting, sort of" in Chapter 6 and "Assorted Files" in Chapter 13 of *UNIX For Dummies*.

spell

Looks through a text file and reports which words are not in the UNIX dictionary.

UNIXspeak

spell [-b] [+*wordlist*] *filenames*

Option or Argument	Function
-b	Uses British spellings
+*wordlist*	Adds the contents of the file named *wordlist* to the UNIX dictionary so that words contained in the *wordlist* file are not considered to be misspelled
filenames	Specifies the file (or files) to be spell-checked

Sample

You have used a text editor to write a memo and you want to check for bogus spelling. You type

```
spell memo.to.bob
```

Tons of words are rejected as misspelled. Then you remember that your friend Harold maintains a "jargon file" of nonstandard words you frequently use. You type

```
spell +/usr/harold/jargon memo.to.bob
```

Many fewer words pop out.

More stuff

spell **works with only text files. If you use a word processor, use its built-in spell-checker instead. Also try running** ipspell**, a nice, free, interactive spell-checker your system administrator may have installed.**

stty

Sets the options for your terminal.

UNIXspeak

stty [*charname char*] [sane] [[-]tostop] [-a]

Option or Argument	Function
charname	Specifies the terminal control character you want to see. Refer to the following table to see what these characters are.
char	Specifies the key (or keys) you want to use for this terminal control character.
sane	Returns your terminal to a "sane" state, which is useful if an editor dies and leaves your terminal in a state in which characters don't echo.
-tostop	Turns off terminal stop mode so that output from background jobs can be displayed on your screen.
tostop	Turns on terminal stop mode, to prevent output from background jobs from being displayed on your screen. (Terminal stop mode is usually on, unless you have turned it off.)
-a	Displays all the terminal settings.

Sample

You want to use Ctrl-Q as the Backspace key on your terminal because it's what you used on your previous system. You type

```
stty erase '^q'
```

Be sure to put quotes around the key name so that stty and the shell don't get confused. The caret (^) means that you press the Ctrl key along with the letter, so '^q' means Ctrl-Q. You type the Delete or Rubout key as '^?'.

To list all your terminal settings, you type

```
stty
```

More stuff

You can change dozens of terminal settings, but you should leave most of them alone. The following table shows terminal control characters you might want to set.

Name	Typical Character	Meaning
erase	Ctrl-H	Erases (backspaces over) the preceding character
kill	Ctrl-U	Discards the line typed so far
eof	Ctrl-D	Marks the end of input to a program
swtch	Ctrl-Z	Pauses the current program
intr	Ctrl-C	Interrupts or kills the current program
quit	Ctrl-\	Kills the current program and writes a core file

To set your terminal options every time you log in, include your stty commands in your .profile, or .login file.

See the section "Setting Up the Terminal the Way You Like It" in Chapter 28 of *UNIX For Dummies*.

---

tail

Displays the last few lines of a file.

UNIXspeak

tail [-r] [-*lines*] *filename*

Option or Argument	Function
-r	Displays the lines in reverse order
-lines	Specifies the number of lines you want to see (counting from the end of the file)
filename	Specifies the file you want to see the end of

Sample

You are wondering whether you remembered to include a P.S. at the end of a memo you wrote. You type

```
tail memo.to.frank
```

You see the last ten lines of the file.

More stuff

Suppose that you maintain a log file of changes to an important database. You want to see the last 20 changes in reverse chronological order, so you type

```
tail -r -20 log.file
```

You can also use tail to see the last lines of output from another command. If you want to see the last ten changes Lydia made to the log file, for example, you can type

```
grep "Lydia" log.file | tail
```

talk

Lets you talk to another computer user by typing messages to each other on-screen.

UNIXspeak

talk *user*[*@computer*]

Option or Argument	Function
user	Specifies the username of the person with whom you want to chat
computer	Specifies the name of the computer on which the person is logged

Sample

You use the finger command to determine that your friend Deb is logged on to the computer system in another building on your campus. According to finger, she is using a computer called samba. To chat with her, you type

    talk deb@samba

Deb sees a message on her screen like this:

    Message from Talk_Daemon@iecc at 2:32 ...
    talk: connection requested by margy@iecc
    talk: respond with: talk margy@iecc

Deb wants to talk with you, so she types

    talk margy@iecc

Now the top part of the screen shows what you type and the bottom part shows what Deb types. (Deb sees the same thing, but vice versa.) You type messages to each other. When you are finished, sign off with a geeky "bibi" or "cul" (see you later) and then press Ctrl-D.

More stuff

To talk to someone on another machine on the network, use the person's electronic-mail address as the computer name. If someone wants to talk to you but you don't want to talk back, you don't have to. When you see the talk message telling you to respond, just don't do it. To prevent people from talking to you at all, type mesg n.

See the section "Can we talk?" in Chapter 17 of *UNIX For Dummies*. *See also* the finger and write commands in this part of the book.

tar

Copies a file to or from an archive file or backup tape or floppy disk.

UNIXspeak

```
tar c|r|t|u|x[l][o][v][w][0-9][f tarfile]
filenames
```

Option or Argument	Function
c	Copies files to a new archive file or tape.
r	Copies files to the end of an existing tape.
t	Displays a list of all the files stored on the tape.
u	Copies files to the tape unless they are already there. If a previous version of a file is on the tape, it copies the new version to the tape (tape only).
x	Copies (extracts) files *from* the archive file or tape.
l	Displays error messages if it cannot find the files you want.
o	When you're extracting files (copying them from the archive file or tape), changes the ownership of the files to you rather than to their original owners.
v	Displays the names of the files as it copies them, plus a (for *a*rchive, when you're copying to an archive file or tape) or x (for e*x*tract, when you're copying from an archive file or tape).
w	Asks you to confirm the copying of each file.
0-9	A single digit says which unit to use. If there's only one tape or floppy, it's unit 0. Check with a local guru to find which value to use.

Option or Argument	Function
f *tarfile*	Specifies the name of the archive file. If the arch is on a disk or tape drive, the name is usually something like /de/ fd096 or /de/tape.
filenames	Specifies the files you want to copy. If you specify directory names, all the files and subdirectories in the directories are included also.

Sample

Someone gives you a tape and tells you that it contains a file you want. The file is called something like mgmt.procedures, and the tape drive is named /de/tape. To find out which files are on the tape, you type

```
tar tvf /de/tape
```

You see that a file is named manager.procedures. Assuming that it is the file you want, you copy it from the tape to the current working directory by typing

```
tar xvf /de/tape manager.procedures
```

You can equally well use tar to create and unpack tar format files, which are often used to pass around a bunch of files on networks. To put all the files in directory project in a tar format file:

```
tar cvf project.tar project
```

and to extract the files from a tar format archive:

```
tar xvf project.tar
```

More stuff

Like disks, tapes can contain directories and subdirectories. You can extract all the files from a directory on a tape. To copy all the files from the /Report directory, for example, you can type

```
tar xvf /de/tape /Report
```

If you use wildcard characters in the filename, be sure to enclose the entire thing in quotes, as shown in the following line, so that tar and the shell don't get confused:

```
tar xvf /de/tape '/Report/*'
```

For information about making and using backups, see the section "Call in the backup squad" in Chapter 22 of *UNIX For Dummies*.

tee

Copies text from a pipe into a file.

UNIXspeak

tee [-a] *filenames*

Option or Argument	Function
-a	Adds material to the end of the files instead of creating them
filenames	Specifies the file (or files) to which to copy material

Sample

You're using the find command to find all your files that haven't been looked at for a month. You want to store the list of files in a new file named stale.files and also see it on-screen. You type

```
find . -atime +30 | tee stale.files
```

More stuff

tee is most useful for making a log of the output of a slow or long-running program while still seeing its output on-screen.

telnet

Lets you log in to a remote computer (see Part VI for details).

time

Tells you how long a command took to run (from the time you pressed Enter or Return to the time you saw the next shell prompt).

UNIXspeak

time ***command*** [*arguments*]

Option or Argument	Function
command	Specifies the command or program you want to run
arguments	Specifies the other information you have to type on the command line

Sample

You are about to run your big, monthly analysis report and you wonder how long it takes to run. You usually type this command to run it:

    agdata 1994-oct

Instead, you use the time command to time it. You type

    time agdata 1994-oct

When the report is finished running, you also see the elapsed time, execution time, and other juicy information about how long the program took.

More stuff

In the C shell, time with no arguments gives the times (elapsed and the amount of the computer's CPU you have used) since the shell began.

The timex command works the same way, except that it provides options for which information to display.

touch

Changes the date and time of a file without changing the file's contents.

UNIXspeak

touch [-a] [-c] [-m] [*date*] ***filenames***

Option or Argument	Function
-a	Changes only the date and time the file was last accessed.
-c	Doesn't create files if they don't already exist. If you use touch without this option on a non-existent filename, it creates an empty file.
-m	Changes only the date and time the file was last modified.
date	Specifies the date and time to give to the file (or files). The date and time must be in the format *mmddhhnn*, where *mm* is the month number, *dd* is the day number, *hh* is the hour (using a 24-hour clock), and *nn* is the minute.
filenames	Specifies the file (or files) whose date (or dates) and time (or times) you want changed.

Sample

You are about to distribute a bunch of files to everyone in your department. Because you may distribute updates later, it would be convenient if all the files had exactly the same modification date and time (the date and time the files were last modified). All the files are stored in the Distrib directory. To set the date and time to noon on Christmas, you type

```
touch 12251200 Distrib/*
```

More stuff

If you leave out the date, touch changes the files' date and time to today, right now.

troff

A baroque but powerful text formatter. troff uses a complex formatting language to format text files for output on a high-quality printer or typesetter. (It stands for *typeset runoff*.)

UNIXspeak

troff [-m*macrofile*] [-n*firstpage*] [-o*pagelist*]
f1lenames

Option or Argument	Function
-m*macrofile*	Specifies the file that contains macros used in the input file
-n*firstpage*	Uses *firstpage* as the page number of the first page that is printed
-o*pagelist*	Specifies the pages you want to print (3-6,15,21, for example)
filenames	Specifies the file (or files) that contains the input text

Sample

Someone gives you a file that has been formatted for use with
troff (that is, a text file that contains troff formatting codes,
more properly called *requests* and *macros*). Luckily, you don't
have to get into the world of troff formatting — you just have to
print the file.

The file is called report6, and you usually use the lp command
to print. You type

    troff report6 | lp

More stuff

Suppose that the paper jammed when it printed page 8, so you
have to print it again. You type

    troff -o8 report6 | lp

When someone gives you a text file formatted for troff, the
printing instructions may say to use a particular *macro file* that
contains macros used by troff. If so, you may need to tell troff
about it when you run it. If you are told to use the ms macros, you
type

    troff -ms report6 | lp

If you want to learn how to format text for use with troff (or its
predecessor, nroff), a useful overview is in *UNIX in a Nutshell*
(O'Reilly & Associates, 1986).

tty

Displays the device name of your terminal.

UNIXspeak

```
tty
```

Sample

You want to know the name of your terminal so that you can report noise on the line to your system administrator. You type

```
tty
```

You see

```
/de/ttyd045
```

More stuff

The terminal ID usually looks like the pathname of a subdirectory of the /de directory. Actually, /de is a directory (it stands for *dev*ice) that contains special files which are really connections to devices such as your terminal, printers, and tape drives.

It's a good idea to know your terminal ID in case something goes wrong. If you have to ask your local UNIX guru for help, you will probably be asked for the terminal ID. Try to sound as though you know what you're talking about: know your terminal ID.

umask

Tells UNIX which permissions to give to files and directories you create.

UNIXspeak

```
umask [permissions]
```

Option or Argument	Function
permissions	Specifies the permissions to give to files you create. Unfortunately, you must specify the permissions as an octal number by using the method described in the next "More stuff" section.

Sample

Generally, when you create new files, you want everyone to be able to read the file but only you and other members of your group to be able to write (edit) them. You therefore type

```
umask 002
```

When you create new files in the future, users who are not in your group aren't able to edit the files.

More stuff

This table shows the numeric codes that make up a umask permission:

Number	Files You Create	Directories You Create
0	Read and write	List files, create files, and cd into directory
1	Read and write	List files and create files
2	Read only	List files and cd into directory
3	Read only	List files
4	Write only	Create files and cd into directory
5	Write only	Create files
6	No access	cd into directory
7	No access	No access

A umask permission consists of three of these numbers: the first, your own permissions; the second, those for your group; and the third, for everyone else. The first number in your umask permission should always be 0 (zero) so that you give yourself complete permissions for everything you create. The most common umasks are 022, to enable anyone to read but only you can write files; 002, to let members of your group change your files and others only to read them; and 077, to let no one but you see any of your files.

You can always change the permissions for your files by using the chmod command, described earlier in this part.

See the section "Mother, May I?" in Chapter 28 of *UNIX For Dummies.*

unalias

C and Korn shells only.

Removes an alias name.

UNIXspeak

unalias *names*

Option or Argument	Function
names	Name (or names) of the aliases you want to delete

Sample

You created an alias for a directory you were using frequently for a project. Now the project is over and you don't want the alias anymore. You type

```
unalias projdir
```

More stuff

See alias for more information about aliases. If you use the Bourne shell, you are out of luck because they don't exist.

uname

Tells you the name of the UNIX system you are using.

UNIXspeak

uname [-s][-a]

Option or Argument	Function
-s	Displays only the system name. If you don't use this option, you get a slew of other information (BSD only).
-a	Displays all system name info (System V only). Without this option, you get just the local system name.

Sample

You want to know the name of your UNIX system so that you can figure out your electronic-mail address. You type

```
uname -s
```

You see the name of the system.

More stuff

To get the complete scoop about your system, you type

```
uname
```

You see

```
plugh plugh 3.2.2 i386
```

You probably will have to ask a UNIX wizard to decode this message for you — it contains version numbers, CPU types, and other technoid info.

---

uncompress

Restores a compressed file to its normal size.

UNIXspeak

uncompress [-c] *filenames*

Option or Argument	Function
-c	Displays the uncompressed version of the file, but doesn't save it as a file or delete the compressed file
filenames	Specifies the compressed files to uncompress

Sample

Someone gives you a compressed file that contains information you want. The file is called facts.Z. The .Z at the end confirms that this file is compressed — if a filename ends with .z instead, it is packed, and you must use the unpack command instead. You type

```
uncompress facts
```

(You can leave the .Z off the filename because uncompress assumes that all compressed files have names that end with .Z.) uncompress creates a new file named facts that contains the uncompressed information from facts.Z. It also deletes facts.Z.

More stuff

If you want to see what is in a compressed file, you can type

    uncompress -c facts

You see the uncompressed contents of the file on-screen, but no new file is created and the compressed file isn't deleted. You can use the zcat command to do the same thing.

To create a compressed file, see the compress command, earlier in this part. Another method of shrinking files uses the pack and unpack commands.

See the section "Squashing Your Files" in Chapter 13 of *UNIX For Dummies*.

---

uniq

Removes repeated identical lines from a text file. If a file contains several adjacent lines that are the same, uniq deletes all but one of them.

UNIXspeak

uniq [-c] [-d] [-u] [-*fields*] [+*chars*] [*existingfile* [*newfile*]]

Option or Argument	Function
-c	Displays each line along with the number of times it occurred
-d	Displays only lines that occurred more than once
-u	Displays only lines that occurred only once
-*fields*	Skips the first *fields* fields on each line (fields are separated by either tabs or spaces) when you're comparing adjacent lines

Option or Argument	Function
+chars	Skips the first *chars* characters on each line when you're comparing adjacent lines
existingfile	Specifies the file that contains the input text
newfile	Specifies the name to use for the new file that contains the output; sends output to the standard output if not specified

Sample

You have an alphabetical list of the book titles in your corporate library, stored one per line in a text file named titles. You think that some titles might have been entered twice. To get rid of possible duplicates, you type

```
uniq titles titles2
```

More stuff

Suppose that you have a text file named visitors that contains a list of the people who used your corporate library this month. The file contains one name per line, with the date preceding each name. You want to know how many times each person visited the library. You type

```
sort visitors | uniq -1 -c > name.list
```

This command line sorts the visitors file so that identical lines are together. Then it runs the uniq command: it skips the first field on each line (the date) and counts the instances of each name. It stashes the output in a file named name.list.

Unless your file is already sorted, you almost always should use sort | uniq rather than just uniq.

unpack

Restores a packed file to its original size.

UNIXspeak

```
unpack filenames
```

Option or Argument	Function
filenames	Specifies the packed files to unpack

Sample

Last year, you saved a file in packed format to save space. Now you want to use the file again. The file is called user.manual.z. The .z at the end confirms that this file is packed — if a filename ends with .Z instead, it is compressed, and you must use the uncompress command instead. You type

```
unpack user.manual.z
```

unpack creates a new file named user.manual that contains the unpacked information from user.manual.z. It also deletes user.manual.z.

More stuff

If you want to see what is in a packed file, you can use the pcat command to display its contents, like this:

```
pcat user.manual
```

You see the unpacked contents of the file on-screen, but no new file is created and the packed file isn't deleted.

To create a packed file, see the pack command. Another method of shrinking files uses the compress and uncompress commands.

See the section "Squashing Your Files" in Chapter 13 of *UNIX For Dummies.*

uudecode

Converts a uuencoded file back into its original form.

UNIXspeak

uudecode ***filename***

Option or Argument	Function
filename	Specifies the name of the uuencoded file

Sample

A friend has sent you a uuencoded program by way of electronic
mail. The message looks something like this:

```
begin 1746 run.me
LKJ3L409DFV13098D.V,,-F=0119208FH
""FLKJEO-19214309 ';'3;L46N-098ASD
```

By using your mail program (see Part V of this book), you save
the message as a text file named uu.incoming. Then you decode
the file by typing

```
uudecode uu.incoming
```

uudecode decodes the file and creates a file named run.me
(the name to use for the decoded file is stored as part of the
uuencoded file). You delete uu.incoming, which you don't want
anymore, and try running the run.me program.

More stuff

uudecode says nothing when it runs unless something went
wrong. You have to look at the input file yourself to find out
the name of the file it decoded.

See the section "Stealing Software from the Network" in Chapter
14 of *UNIX For Dummies*.

uuencode

Disguises a program as a text file so that you can send it through
electronic mail.

UNIXspeak

uuencode *existingfile decodedname*

Option or Argument	Function
existingfile	Specifies the program (or other file) you want to disguise as a text file
decodedname	Specifies the name to be used later for the uudecoded file, after the file is mailed

Sample

Your programming staff has written a fabulous new program you want to share with a few friends. The program is currently called `fish.squish`, but when your friends receive it, you want it to be called `run.me`. You type

```
uuencode fish.squish run.me > file.to.send
```

`uuencode` creates a uuencoded file named `file.to.send`, in which the program has been transformed into a meaningless jumble of letters, numbers, and punctuation. You send the file to your friends by using electronic mail. When they use `uudecode` (described earlier in this part) on this file, it creates a file named `run.me` that contains the runnable program.

More stuff

You can encode and mail your program in one fell swoop, like this:

```
uuencode fish.squish run.me | mail
jordan@carioca
```

This command line uuencodes the file and mails it to your friend Jordan.

 See the section "Stealing Software from the Network" in Chapter 14 of *UNIX For Dummies.*

---

vacation

 Automatically responds to incoming electronic-mail messages by telling people that you are on vacation. (This command does not exist on all UNIX systems.)

UNIXspeak

vacation [-l] [-m] [-M *filename*]

Option or Argument	Function
-l	Stores the names of people who send you messages while you were away. The names are stored in a file named `.maillog` in your home directory.

Option or Argument	Function
-m	Stores all the messages you received while you were away. The messages are stored in a file named `.mailfile` in your home directory.
-M *filename*	Sends the message in *filename* rather than the standard vacation message.

Sample

You are about to go on your annual two-week pilgrimage to Fiji, and you want people to know it. You type

```
vacation -m
```

Now any messages you receive are responded to automatically with a message which says that you're away on vacation. The wording of the response varies from one version of the vacation program to another.

More stuff

Sooner or later, however, you must come back. When you get back to your desk, cancel the `vacation` command by typing

```
mail -F ""
```

(This command stops your mail from being forwarded to the `vacation` program.)

vi

Runs a powerful but yucky screen-oriented text editor. See Part IV to learn how to use it, or preferably how to use a better text editor, such as `emacs`.

See also the section "Shy `vi`, the princess of text editors" in Chapter 12 of *UNIX For Dummies*.

wc

Counts the number of words, lines, and characters in a file.

UNIXspeak

wc `[-c] [-l] [-w]` *filename*

Option or Argument	Function
-c	Displays only the number of characters in the file
-l	Displays only the number of lines in the file
-w	Displays only the number of words in the file
filename	Specifies the name of the text file to count

Sample

You have spent two days working on an essay that is supposed to be no longer than 1,000 words. You type

```
wc my.essay
```

You see the number of characters, words, and lines in the file. If you want only the word count, you type

```
wc -w my.essay
```

More stuff

You can use `wc` to count the output of other commands. If you are wondering, for example, how many files you have in your home directory and its subdirectories, you can type

```
find . -print | wc -w
```

This command finds all the files (beginning with the current directory) in the directory and its subdirectories. The output of the `find` command (the list of filenames) becomes the input to the `wc` command.

---

who

Tells you who else is using this computer.

UNIXspeak

who `[-q]` `[am i]`

Option or Argument	Function
-q	Displays only usernames, not terminal IDs or other information
am i	Displays your username, in case you have forgotten or if you have walked up to a terminal that someone left logged in

Sample

You are wondering why your computer is so slow today. To find out who is using it, you type

`who`

You see a list of usernames, terminal IDs, and login times.

More stuff

The `users` command displays a list of the users who are currently logged in. On some systems, you can type `whoami` rather than `who am i` to find out your username. *See also* the `finger` command to get more information about who is on your computer or on the network.

See the section "Finding Out Who's on Your Computer" in Chapter 17 of *UNIX For Dummies.*

---

write

Displays a message on the screen of another user.

UNIXspeak

write *username* [*terminal*]

Option or Argument	Function
username	Specifies the person to whom you want to send a message.

Option or Argument	Function
terminal	Specifies the terminal the person is using. You have to mention this option only if the person is using several terminals (or terminal windows) at the same time.

Sample

You want to send an important message to your friend Dave, who works down the hall. You type

```
write dave
```

UNIX says nothing, so you type the message and press Enter or Return at the end of each line:

```
Dave, it's Margy!
What about going out for some tacos?
```

At the end of the message, you press Ctrl-D. The message appears on Dave's screen.

More stuff

Sometimes write tells you something like this:

```
dave is logged on more than one place
You are connected to "vt01".
Other locations are:
ttyp1
ttyp0
```

Which terminal is Dave using? In reality, Dave is probably using only one terminal and is probably using several xterm windows under Motif (see xterm later in this part and Part III, "Using Motif"). Use the finger command to figure out which "terminal" is the one your friend is using.

See also talk. Better yet, use electronic mail (see Part V).

Antisocial (or busy) users can turn off writes to their screen by using the mesg command.

See the section "Chatting with Other People on Your Computer" in Chapter 17 of *UNIX For Dummies*.

Part III

Using Motif

Window managers

Window managers are programs that control the way your screen is set up. Several managers are used on UNIX systems. Motif is by far the most popular, but others are still in use, such as OPEN LOOK.

If you're stuck with a window manager other than Motif, see Chapter 11 of *UNIX For Dummies* for details.

Clicking the mouse

When you click the mouse, you point at or select something on your screen.

Steps

1. Move the cursor to the place you want to select.

2. Quickly press and release a mouse button. UNIX mice usually have three buttons; unless you're directed otherwise, you use the leftmost button.

3. The cursor moves to the location where you clicked.

More stuff

Some programs need double- or triple-clicks — that is, you click the mouse twice or three times in rapid succession. You may have to practice to be able to click fast enough for it to see one double click rather than two single clicks.

Dragging the mouse

When you drag your mouse (poor thing!), you move an object from one place to another.

Steps

1. Move the cursor to the thing you want to move.

2. Press the mouse button and hold it down.

3. While keeping the button pressed, move the cursor to the place to which you want to drag the item.

4. Let go of the button.

Selecting a bunch of stuff

By selecting a bunch of stuff, you select an area, such as a chunk of text in a window.

Steps

1. Move the cursor to the beginning of the area you want to select.

2. Press the mouse button and hold it down.

3. While keeping the mouse button pressed, move the cursor to the end of what you want to select. The selected material changes color as you do this step.

4. Release the button.

See the section "Basic Mouse Skills" in Chapter 10 of *UNIX For Dummies*.

Window anatomy

Each Motif window is surrounded by a border that contains lots of exciting pieces:

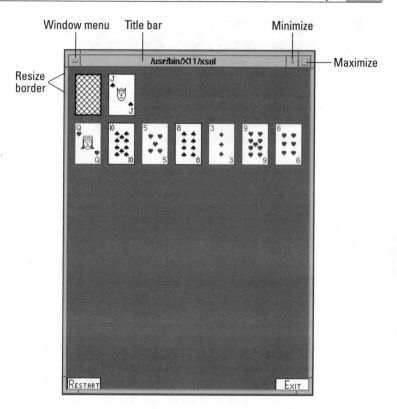

Name	*Use*
Window menu	Displays the Window menu
Title bar	Moves, resizes, and so on
Minimize	Turns the window into an icon
Maximize	Makes the window fill the screen
Resize border	Changes the size of the window

Switching windows

When you switch windows, you select which window is the *active* window, the window that receives text you type from the keyboard. Motif makes the border around the active window a different color from the others. Depending on your setup, you use one of these ways to switch windows:

- *Click-to-type:* Move the mouse to the window you want and click the mouse anywhere in that window.

- *Move-to-type:* Although it's not standard Motif (but quite popular), you merely move the mouse to the window you want to use.

 To tell which way you select a window, move your mouse from one window to another without clicking. If the window borders change colors, you have move-to-type. If not, it's click-to-type.

 You can bring any window to the front (that is, make it so that no other overlapping window obscures it), by clicking anywhere in the window's frame or by moving to the window and pressing Alt-F1.

Keyboard shortcuts

Keyboard shortcuts are the keyboard equivalents of mouse actions, for the rodent-impaired who don't have a mouse or don't want to use it:

Key	Action
Alt-F1	Brings window to front, on top of any others
Alt-F3	Drops the active window to the rear, behind any others
Alt-F4	Closes the active window
Alt-F5	Restores an iconified window
Alt-F6	Switches to the next window
Alt-F7	Moves the active window
Alt-F8	Changes the size of the active window
Alt-F9	Minimizes the active window to an icon
Alt-F10	Maximizes the active window to fill the entire screen

Key	Action
Shift-Esc	Displays the window menu (described later in this part of the book)
Alt-Space	Displays the window menu
Alt-Tab	Switches to the next window
Alt-Shift-Tab	Switches to the preceding window

More stuff

Your system manager, if she's in a perverse mood, can change any or all of the keyboard and mouse commands to anything else she wants. If you try some of these commands and the wrong thing happens, and you're absolutely sure that you typed or moused the right thing, you may be a victim of excessive customization. You have to inquire locally to get the details.

If you're familiar with Microsoft Windows, you will notice that these key combinations are about the same as the ones Windows uses.

The window menu

In the window menu (see the following figure), you perform standard window operations, such as changing the size, moving the window, and minimizing the window to an icon. You display the window menu in one of three ways:

- Click the little bar in the upper left corner with the first mouse button.

- Click anywhere in the window border with the second mouse button.

- Press Shift-Esc or Alt-spacebar.

Restore	Alt+F5
Front	Alt+F1
Move	Alt+F7
Size	Alt+F8
Minimize	Alt+F9
Maximize	Alt+F10
Lower	Alt+F3
Close	Alt+F4

The window menu lists the most common window operations along with the shortcut keys. Operations that aren't currently valid (Restore, for example, in the menu in the picture) are grayed out. You can select any of the menu entries in three ways:

- Click the menu entry with the mouse.

- Type the underlined letter in the menu entry.

- Press the shortcut key combination.

More stuff

Icons (see the following section) have window menus also, which you display in much the same way: click the icon with the first mouse button, or click and hold the second mouse button, or press Shift-Esc or Alt-spacebar.

You can always use the shortcut key combination regardless of whether the window menu is displayed. If you do a great deal of window wrangling, the shortcut keys are the easiest way to do many window operations.

Mouse lovers can display the window menu and select an entry in one operation: move the cursor to the bar in the upper left corner and press and hold the mouse button. When the menu appears, move the cursor to the entry you want and release the button. This menu, known as a *pull-down menu,* is used in lots of applications, including Motif.

A user-friendly way to open windows

Steps

1. Move the mouse to a part of the screen outside any window.

2. Press the mouse button. If you have large windows, you may have to move one to get some clear screen area. When you press the mouse button, a "root" menu appears (see the following figure). With luck, it has an entry for the menu you want.

Several user-friendly shell programs also provide icons for popular programs; if you have one of these programs, click the appropriate icon.

An obsolete but easy way to open windows

Steps

1. Switch to a window running the UNIX shell.

2. Type as a UNIX command the name of the program you want to run. Shazam.

See the section "Opening a New Window" in Chapter 11 of *UNIX For Dummies*.

Minimizing windows

When you minimize a window, you shrink it to an icon, which is a little box on-screen that represents the window (see the following figure). From the icon, you can *restore* the window to its original state, with any running program just where it was when you minimized it. You can minimize a window in one of three ways:

• Click its minimize button, the little dot near the upper right.

• Select Minimize from the window menu.

• Press Alt-F9.

Restoring windows from icons

You restore windows from icons by expanding the icon back to the window that appeared before you iconized it. You must restore a window before you can use the program. Use one of these three ways:

- On the icon's window menu, select <u>R</u>estore.
- Double-click on the icon with the first button.
- Move to the icon and press Alt-F5.

Maximizing windows

To maximize a window, you expand it until it fills the entire screen. To maximize a window:

- Click its maximize button, the little block to the right of the minimize button.
- Select Ma<u>x</u>imize from the window menu.
- Press Alt-F10.

Unmaximizing windows

When you unmaximize a window, you return it to its previous size. To unmaximize a window:

- Click the maximize button again.
- Select <u>R</u>estore from the window menu.
- Press Alt-F5.

Changing window sizes

You can change the size and shape of a window by using either the mouse or the keyboard.

Steps

1. Move the mouse to the window border.
2. Drag the border to make the window the size you want. The side borders move left and right, the top and bottom borders move up and down, and the corners move in all four directions.

Real mouse haters use the keyboard:

1. Press Alt-F8 to put the window in "resize mode."

2. Press the cursor keys to change the window size. Holding down the Ctrl key while you press the cursor keys changes the size in larger steps.

3. Press Enter to accept the new size; press Esc to return to the old size.

Moving windows

You can change the position of a window without changing its size. You can use the mouse, the keyboard, or both.

Steps

1. Move the mouse to the title area, the wide part of the top border that shows the name of the window.

2. Press and hold the mouse button.

3. Drag the window to where you want it.

4. Release the button.

Using the keyboard:

1. Press Alt-F7 to put the window in "move mode."

2. Press the cursor keys to move the window. Holding down the Ctrl key while using the cursor keys moves the window in larger steps.

3. Press Enter to accept the new position or press Esc to return to the old place.

More stuff

You can move a window off the edge of the screen if you want to get it out of the way for a minute. When you move the window back to the screen, the part that fell off the screen comes back as good as new.

Exiting Motif

Exiting Motif means leaving the Motif window manager and returning to the UNIX shell. Depending on how your version of Motif was set up, you exit in one of two ways.

Steps

If you have a window called `login`:

1. Switch to that window. The window contains a UNIX shell.

2. Type **exit** or **logout** to exit from the shell; Motif takes the hint and shuts down.

Otherwise:

1. Display the root menu by moving the mouse outside any window and pressing a button.

2. Select the command called Quit or Exit on the root menu.

More stuff

When you leave Motif, it blows away every program running in every window without giving them a chance to save your work. Clean up before you exit.

See the section "Ta-Ta for Now" in Chapter 11 of *UNIX For Dummies*.

Part IV

Using Text Editors

Starting ed

ed is an old-fashioned line editor used to edit text files, including writing electronic-mail messages or shell scripts. Because screen editors are much easier to use (see the information about vi and emacs later in this part of the book), use ed only if you are stuck in it.

Steps

1. In the UNIX shell, type

   ed *filename*

2. If the file already exists, you see the number of characters in it. If you are creating a new file, you see a question mark.

More stuff

All ed commands consist of one letter. Be sure to use the same capitalization shown in the section called "ed commands" later in this part — most basic ed commands are lowercase.

ed thinks of your text file as a bunch of lines of text, and commands work with one line at a time. ed commands are listed later in this part of the book. The line you are currently using is called the *current line*, and commands apply to that line unless you tell them otherwise.

To complicate matters, ed is always either in command mode or input mode. In *command mode*, letters you type are interpreted as commands. In *input mode*, what you type is entered in the file you are editing.

To make ed more livable, type **P** (that's a capital P) to put it in
prompt mode so that it displays an asterisk whenever it is in
command mode and waiting for a command. Then type **H** to tell
ed to display more helpful messages when something goes wrong.

See the section "Talk to Mr. ed" in Chapter 12 of *UNIX For Dummies*.

Getting out of ed

The sooner, the better, we think!

1. If you are in input mode, type a period and press Enter to
   get into command mode.

2. Type **w** to save your work (unless you don't want to).

3. Type **q** to quit the program. You see the shell prompt again.

More stuff

If you want to exit from ed without saving the changes you have
made to the file, type **q**. When ed displays a question mark, type **q**
again.

ed *commands*

Command	What It Does
a	Appends text (that is, adds a line after the current line and switches to input mode). To exit from input mode and return to command mode, type a period on a line by itself.
*n*a	Appends text after line number *n*.
d	Deletes current line.
*n*d	Deletes line number *n*.
*n,m*d	Deletes lines numbered *n* through *m*.
h	Displays a help message right now.
H	Displays help messages whenever anything goes wrong.
i	Inserts text (that is, inserts a line before the current line and switches to input mode). To exit from input mode and return to command mode, type a period on a line by itself.

Command	What It Does
*n*i	Inserts text before line number *n*.
n	Displays the current line with a line number.
*n,m*n	Displays lines numbered *n* through *m* with line numbers.
1,$n	Displays all the lines in the file with line numbers.
p	Displays the current line without line numbers (we recommend using the n command instead because you have to know line numbers to edit the lines).
*n,m*p	Displays lines numbered *n* through *m* without line numbers.
1,$p	Displays all the lines in the file without line numbers.
P	Displays an asterisk whenever ed is in command mode.
q	Quits the program.
Q	Quits even if changes haven't been saved.
s/*text1*/*text2*/	Substitutes *text2* for *text1* the first place it appears in the current line.
s/*text1*/*text2*/g	Substitutes *text2* for *text1* everywhere it appears in the current line.
*n,m*s/*text1*/*text2*/	Substitutes *text2* for *text1* the first place it appears in each line numbered *n* through *m*.
*n,m*s/*text1*/*text2*/	Substitutes *text2* for *text1* everywhere it appears in each line numbered *n* through *m*.
u	Undoes the last change you made.
w	Writes (saves) the file.
Enter (the Enter or Return key)	Displays the next line of the file.
. (period)	Displays the next line of the file. In input mode, a period on a line by itself returns to command mode.

There are lots of other ed commands — in fact, almost every letter is a command. So watch out what you type while you are in command mode!

Starting vi

Steps

vi is a widely used, powerful screen editor used to edit text files, including writing electronic-mail messages or shell scripts. vi uses more or less the same commands as ed does.

1. In the UNIX shell, type

   vi *filename*

2. vi displays the first screen of the file. If the file isn't long enough to fill the screen, vi shows tildes (~) on the blank lines. The cursor is at the beginning of the file. The bottom line of the screen shows the filename and the size of the file.

More stuff

Like ed commands, all vi commands are one letter and are listed later in this part of the book.

Be sure to use either capital or small letters as shown in the section "vi commands" — in many cases, a capital letter does something rather different from the same small letter!

Also like ed, vi is always either in command mode or input mode (also called *insert mode*). In *command mode*, letters you type are interpreted as commands. In *input mode*, what you type is entered in the file you are editing.

To switch from command mode to input mode, you give an a or i command (described later in this part) to tell vi where to input the new text.

To switch from input mode to command mode, press the Esc key. Press it a few times, just to be sure. (vi just beeps when you press Esc when you are already in command mode.)

To run a friendlier version of vi, try typing **vedit** rather than **vi** to edit a file. The vedit program displays various helpful messages, including messages that tell you when you are in input or command mode.

See the section "Shy vi, the princess of text editors" in Chapter 12 of *UNIX for Dummies*.

Getting out of vi

1. If you are in input mode, press the Esc key to get into command mode.

2. Type **:w** and then press Enter to save your work (unless you don't want to).

3. Type **ZZ** to quit the program (those are capital Zs). You see the shell prompt again.

More stuff

If you want to exit from vi without saving the changes you have made to the file, type **:q!** to quit without saving.

vi *commands*

Command	What It Does
Esc	Returns to command mode from input mode. In command mode, it just beeps.
Enter	Moves to the beginning of the next line.
0	Moves to the beginning of the current line.
$	Moves to the end of the current line.
+	Moves to the beginning of the next line.
-	Moves to the beginning of the preceding line.
)	Moves the cursor to the beginning of the next sentence. (A sentence ends with a period, exclamation point, or question mark followed by two spaces.)
(	Moves the cursor to the beginning of the current sentence.
}	Moves the cursor to the beginning of the next paragraph. (A paragraph ends with a blank line.)
{	Moves the cursor to the beginning of the current paragraph.
/text	Searches forward through the file for the text.
/	Repeats the same search, searching forward.
?	Repeats the same search, searching backward.
:!command	Runs a shell command and then returns to vi.
a	Adds text (that is, switches to input mode so that the text you type is added immediately after the cursor).
A	Adds text at the end of the current line, switching to input mode.

Command	What It Does
b or B	Moves the cursor backward one word.
dd	Deletes the entire current line.
*n*dd	Deletes the next *n* lines.
D	Deletes the text from the cursor to the end of the line.
d^	Deletes the text from the cursor to the beginning of the line.
dw	Deletes the next word.
d)	Deletes to the end of the sentence.
d}	Deletes to the end of the paragraph.
dG	Deletes to the end of the file. (Watch out!)
e or E	Moves the cursor to the end of the word.
G	Goes (moves the cursor) to the end of the file.
1G (that's a one.)	Moves the cursor to the beginning of the file.
h	Moves the cursor left one character.
H	Moves the cursor to the top line of the screen.
i	Inserts text (that is, switches to input mode so that the text you type is inserted immediately before the cursor).
I	Inserts text at the beginning of the current line, switching to input mode.
j	Moves the cursor down one line.
k	Moves the cursor up one line.
l	Moves the cursor right one character.
L	Moves the cursor to the bottom line of the screen.
n	Repeats the last search (made with /).
N	Repeats the last search (made with /), searching in the opposite direction.
o	Opens (creates) a new line after the current line, switching to input mode so that you can type text on it.
O (the capital letter , not a zero)	Opens a new line before the current line, switching to input mode so that you can type text on it.
p	Inserts ("puts") text deleted by the last y or Y command. The text is added just after the cursor.

Command	What It Does
P	Inserts text deleted by the last y or Y command, just before the cursor.
:q! (followed by Enter)	Exits from the program without saving your changes.
R	Replaces text, switching to input mode so that the text you type replaces the text that is currently to the right of the cursor (also called *overtype* mode).
:sh	Runs the shell while putting vi on hold. To return from the shell, type **exit** or press Ctrl-D. You return to vi with the same file loaded and your cursor in the same position. Be sure to save your file before trying this command.
u	Undoes the last change.
U	Undoes all changes to the current line since you moved to the line.
w or W	Moves the cursor forward one word.
x	Deletes the character to the right of the cursor.
X	Deletes the character to the left of the cursor.
:x (followed by Enter)	Exits from vi and saves any changes to the file.
*n*x	Deletes the next *n* characters.
*n*X	Deletes the previous *n* characters.
:w (followed by Enter)	Writes (saves) the file.
yy	Copies ("yanks") the current line to a buffer for later use.
yw	Copies the current word to a buffer for later use.
y)	Copies the current sentence to a buffer for later use.
y}	Copies the current paragraph to a buffer for later use.
Y	Same as yy.
ZZ	Exits from vi after saving any changes to the file.
Ctrl-B	Scrolls backward one screen.
Ctrl-F	Scrolls forward one screen.
Ctrl-Z	Suspends vi and returns to the UNIX shell. Works only if your UNIX shell handles job control. Resume vi by typing **fg**.

Command	What It Does
ed command	You can do any ed command in vi by typing a colon and the ed command and then pressing Enter.

There are lots of other vi commands — in fact, almost every letter is a command. So watch out what you type while you are in command mode! And be sure to use capital and small letters in commands just as they are listed in the table!

vi *commands in input mode*

Command	What It Does
Esc	Returns to command mode from input mode (Ctrl-C does this too).
Ctrl-B	Scrolls backward one screen.
Ctrl-F	Scrolls forward one screen.
Ctrl-H	Backspaces.
Ctrl-J	Moves the cursor down one line (Ctrl-N also does this).
Ctrl-L	Redisplays the text on the screen (Ctrl-R also does this).
Ctrl-P	Moves the cursor up one line.
Ctrl-W	Moves the cursor backward to the beginning of the word.

Starting emacs

emacs is used to edit text files, including writing electronic-mail messages or shell scripts.

Steps

1. In the UNIX shell, type

   emacs *filename*

2. emacs displays the first screen of the file. The cursor is at the beginning of the file. The bottom line of the screen shows the filename and other information.

More stuff

On some systems, the emacs program is named e or gmacs or epsilon. Some UNIX installations don't have emacs — nag your system administrator to get it!

Unlike the ed and vi programs described earlier, emacs doesn't have input and command modes. To type text, just type it. You type commands by using various combinations of the Ctrl and Meta keys. Unfortunately, your keyboard is unlikely to have a key marked "Meta," so use the Alt key instead. If you don't have an Alt key, press the Esc key and then the key (or keys) to Meta-fy.

See the section "A novel concept in editing: emacs makes sense" in Chapter 12 of *UNIX for Dummies*.

Getting out of emacs

Steps

1. Save your work by pressing Ctrl-X, Ctrl-S.

2. Exit from emacs by typing Ctrl-X, Ctrl-C. You see the shell prompt.

emacs *commands*

Command	What It Does
Meta-< (Meta-Shift-comma)	Moves the cursor to the beginning of the file.
Meta->	Moves the cursor to the end of the file.
Meta-%	Replaces all occurrences of one piece of text with another. emacs asks you for the text to be replaced and the text to replace it with.
Ctrl-@ (Ctrl-Shift-2)	Puts a *mark* at the cursor location. After you move the cursor, you can move or copy the text between the mark and the cursor by using the Ctrl-W or Meta-W keystroke.
Ctrl-A	Moves the cursor to the beginning of the line.
Ctrl-B	Moves the cursor back one character.
Meta-B	Moves the cursor back one word.
Ctrl-D	Deletes the character to the right of the cursor.

Command	What It Does
Meta-D	Deletes the current word.
Ctrl-E	Moves the cursor to the end of the line.
Ctrl-F	Moves the cursor forward one character.
Meta-F	Moves the cursor forward one word.
Ctrl-G	Cancels the current command.
Ctrl-H	Enters the on-line help system.
Ctrl-H C	Displays the command that is run when you press a particular key.
Ctrl-H T	Runs a tutorial about emacs.
Ctrl-K	Deletes ("kills") the text from the cursor to the end of the line and stores it in the *kill buffer*.
Ctrl-N	Moves the cursor to the next line.
Ctrl-P	Moves the cursor to the preceding line.
Meta-Q	Reformats the current paragraph, using word wrap, so that the lines are full.
Ctrl-S	Searches for text. As you type the text, emacs homes in on it. When you find what you are looking for, press Esc or move the cursor. To repeat the search, press Ctrl-S again.
Meta-S	Centers the current line.
Ctrl-T	Transposes the two characters before the cursor.
Meta-T	Transposes the two words before the cursor.
Meta-U	Capitalizes all the letters of the current word.
Ctrl-V	Scrolls down one screen.
Meta-V	Scrolls up one screen.
Ctrl-W	Deletes ("whomps") the text between the mark (set by using Ctrl-@) and the cursor and stores it in the kill buffer. To get it back, press Ctrl-Y.
Meta-W	Copies the text between the mark and the cursor to the kill buffer so that you can insert copies of it by using Ctrl-Y.
Ctrl-X Ctrl-C	Exits from emacs.
Ctrl-X Ctrl-S	Saves the file.
Ctrl-X Ctrl-U	Undoes the last change.

Command	What It Does
Ctrl-X doctor (followed by Enter)	Stops doing useful work and starts "doctor mode," playing a game in which emacs acts as a Rogerian psychologist, responding to your statements with questions. Save your work first. Not in all versions of emacs, unfortunately.
Ctrl-Y	Inserts ("yanks") the text that is in the kill buffer and places it after the cursor.
Del (the Del key)	Deletes the character before the cursor.
Meta-Del	Deletes the word in front of the cursor.

emacs *commands for editing multiple files*

Used for editing several files at the same time and for viewing several files on-screen. Each file is edited in an emacs *buffer* and is visible in a *window*.

Command	What It Does
Ctrl-X B	Switches to a different buffer for editing.
Ctrl-X Ctrl-F	Finds a file and reads it into a buffer for editing.
Ctrl-X K	Closes this buffer. If you haven't saved the file it contains, emacs asks you what to do.
Ctrl-X Ctrl-I	Inserts a file into the current file at the cursor position.
Ctrl-X O	Switches to the other window.
Ctrl-X Ctrl-S	Saves the current buffer into its file.
Ctrl-X 1	Unsplits the screen so that only one window is visible. This command doesn't close any buffers.
Ctrl-X 2	Splits the screen into two windows so that you can view two files at the same time.

Part V

Sending and Receiving Mail

Every UNIX system comes with some sort of mail system. At worst, you have a primitive mail program and can send mail only to other users on your machine. At best, you have a much better mail program (probably `elm`) and can send mail to anyone on the global Internet.

Addressing your mail

When you address your mail, you enter the *mail address* of the person to whom you want to send mail. Every user has a mail address, usually the same as your user (login) name. If your computer is attached to a network, your mail address is your user name, an at sign (@), and the name of your computer (`betsy@marketing`, for example). Some systems using the ancient `uucp` network software use an exclamation point, as in `marketing!betsy`. System administrators can set up other mail addresses for mailing lists, remote users, and other special purposes.

See the section "Addressing the Mail" in Chapter 18 of *UNIX for Dummies*.

Running the `Mail` program

The `Mail` program is the basic, old Berkeley mail program that comes with all UNIX systems. It may be named `mail`, or it might be `mailx` or `Mail`. You use the same program to send and to receive mail, with different arguments.

If your system has `mailx` or `Mail`, there may be another, even older `mail` program you don't want to use.

Sending messages with Mail

Steps

1. Run your mail program and give it the name (or names) of the mail recipients. (In our examples, we use the Mail program: substitute mail or mailx if you use them.)

   Mail elvis@ntw.org

2. Depending on how the mail program has been configured, it may prompt you for a subject line; if so, type one:

   Subject: **Hound dogs**

   If it doesn't ask for a subject and you want to provide one, type ~s followed by the subject:

   ~sHound dogs

3. Type your message.

4. When you're finished, type a dot on a line by itself. The mail program responds with "EOT." (Some ancient versions don't understand the dot; for them, press Ctrl-D. UNIX sends the message.)

More stuff

While you're sending mail, these commands are available. Each starts with a tilde on a new, blank line:

Command	What It Does
~b *name*	Adds a name to the blind carbon-copy list
~c *name*	Adds a name to the blind copy list
~e	Runs a text editor (usually vi) to edit the message
~f	Forwards the current message from the mailbox to someone else
~p	Prints (displays on-screen) the message so far
~q	Quits and abandons this message
~r *file*	Reads in the contents of *file*
~s *subject*	Sets the message subject
~c *name*	Adds a name to the list of recipients
~v	Visual edit: runs the vi editor to edit the message
~w *file*	Writes the message so far to a file
~.	Ends the message and delivers it

> **TIP** If you want to save a copy of a message you are sending, be sure to include your own user name in the blind carbon-copy list, by using the ~b command.

Reading your mail with `Mail`

Steps

1. Run your mail program by typing `Mail`, `mail`, or `mailx`. It shows you your new messages followed by a question mark prompt, like this:

```
mailx version 3.1  Type ? for help.
"/usr/mail/johnl": 21 messages 1 new
>N 21 elvis     Thu Dec 16 15:59    17/361
Club date ?
```

2. To read each new message, press Enter.

3. After reading a message, decide whether you want to save it. To delete it, type **d**, or **dp** to delete it and display the next message. To keep it, press Enter to display the next message.

Printing messages with `Mail`

The `Mail` program doesn't have a built-in printing command, but it's easy to fake it. Just tell it to send the message to the standard printing program. Within the `Mail` program, on BSD UNIX systems, type **| lpr**.

(That's a vertical bar, a space, and the `lpr` command.)

On UNIX System V, type **| lp**.

Saving messages with `Mail`

With `Mail`, you can store messages in a text file for later perusal, editing, printing, or other uses.

Steps

1. Run your mail program. It shows you your new messages.

2. Select the message you want, either by pressing Enter until it shows the message you want or by typing the message number and then pressing Enter.

3. Type **s**, a space, and the name of the file in which to save the message.

You can save as many messages as you want in a single file. That file can be treated as a mailbox; use `Mail -f filename` to tell `Mail` to read its contents.

Exiting from the `Mail` program

Type **q** to quit and save changes to your mailbox.

Type **x** to exit and discard changes to your mailbox.

See the section "Playing Postman Pat with `mail`" in Chapter 18 of *UNIX for Dummies.*

`Mail` command-line options

UNIX'speak

```
mail [-e][-f file][-N][-H][-s subject][recipients]
```

Option or Argument	Function
-e	Just tells you whether there's any new mail, without displaying it.
-f *file*	Reads your mail from the mailbox file you specify.
-N	Doesn't list message headers when it starts.
-H	Lists only the messages headers and then exits.
-s *subject*	Sets the subject when sending mail.
recipients	Sets the name (or names) of recipient (or recipients) when you're sending mail.

Using the `elm` program

The `elm` mail program is widely used and much easier to use.

Some systems use `pine`, a simpler `elm`-like program. The same commands work, so read on.

Running the elm *program*

Type elm. You see the *message index*, a nice listing of your messages with one message per line. At the bottom of the screen is a list of elm commands you can use.

Sending messages with elm

Steps

1. Run elm.

2. Type **m** to send a message.

3. elm asks who to send the message to. Type a mail address.

4. elm prompts you for the message subject. Type it in.

5. elm may ask for addresses to which you want to send copies of the message. Type the names if there are any. (Type your own username if you want to keep a copy for yourself.) Just press Enter or Return if you don't want to send any copies.

6. elm runs a text editor, usually vi. Type your message.

7. In the editor, give the commands to save the completed message and exit from the editor. In vi, type **ZZ** or **:x**. In emacs, press Ctrl-X, Ctrl-S, Ctrl-X, Ctrl-C.

8. elm asks something like this:

   ```
   Please choose one of the following options
   by parenthesized letter:

   e)dit message, !)shell, h)eaders,
   c)opy file, s)end, or f)orget.
   ```

   You have the choice of typing **s** to send the message, **h** to edit the header lines, **e** to go back and edit the message some more, **c** to copy a file into the message, **!** to run a shell command, or **f** to forget it and throw away the message.

9. To send the message, type **s**. elm sends the message and displays the list of messages in your mailbox again.

If you hate vi as much as we do, ask your system administrator to set up your copy of elm to run emacs instead or the text editor of your choice, or see the section "Changing your elm options" at the end of this part of the book.

Reading your mail with `elm`

Steps

1. Run `elm`. It shows you the message index.

2. Press the cursor keys to move the cursor to the message you want. If the message is off the bottom of the screen (because you have more messages than can fit, you popular person), press the spacebar to see each subsequent screen of messages or use the cursor keys to scroll through the list.

3. Press Enter to view the message. If the message is too long to fit on-screen, press the spacebar to see more of it.

4. When you finish reading the message, decide whether you want to keep it. Type **d** to delete the message and go on to the next one. To keep it, press the cursor up- or down-arrow keys to go to previous or subsequent messages without deleting anything.

5. To stop reading messages, type **i** to return to the message index.

Printing messages with `elm`

Steps

1. Run `elm`. It shows you the message index.

2. Press the cursor keys to select the message you want to print.

3. Press **p**. That was simple, wasn't it?

Saving messages with `elm`

You can use `elm` to store messages in a text file for later perusal, editing, printing, or other uses.

Steps

1. Run `elm`. It shows you the message index.

2. Press the cursor keys to select the message you want to save.

3. Press **s**.

4. Type the name of the file in which to save the message or press Enter to accept `elm`'s suggested filename (usually the name of the sender).

TIP

Your mailbox usually resides in a subdirectory of your home directory called Mail. If you precede a filename with an equal sign, such as =loveletters, elm knows that you want the file to be in your Mail directory. You can save multiple messages into one file: elm just adds the new messages to the end.

Exiting from the elm program

To quit elm and save any changes you have made to your mailbox, such as deleting messages:

1. Type **q**.

2. elm asks whether you want to save messages you've already read. Type **y** or press Enter to save them in a file named received) or press **n** to leave them in your mailbox. Either way, your messages are saved in one place or the other.

To quit elm without saving changes to your mailbox:

1. Type **x**.

2. If you've made changes, elm asks whether that's what you really want to do.

REFERENCE

3. Type **y** or **n**.

See the section "Playing Postman Pat with elm" in Chapter 18 of *UNIX for Dummies*.

Changing your elm options

You can customize elm so that it uses the editor you like, displays the message in the order you want, and other nifty things.

Steps

1. Run elm. It shows you the message index.

2. To see your elm options, press **o**. elm displays a list of its options, along with your setting for each one. Most of these settings should be left alone so that you don't break elm.

3. To use a different editor for composing messages, type **e**. Your cursor jumps to the name of the editor that elm currently runs when you want to send a message. Edit this program name and press Enter. Notice that it is a full pathname: ask your system administrator to tell you the full pathname of the editor you want to use. Then press Enter.

4. To change the order in which messages are displayed in the message index, type **s**. Then press the spacebar repeatedly until you see the ordering you want. Press **r** to switch between forward and reverse orders. (Our favorite is "Date Mail Sent," sorting from least recent to most recent.) Then press Enter.

5. To change other settings, press the letter that appears in front of the parenthesis at the beginning of its line. Make the change and press Enter.

6. When you finish messing around, press > to save these changes. If you think that you might have made a mistake, skip this step.

7. To return to your elm message index, press **i**.

Getting help in elm

To see some terse but useful on-line help in elm, type a question mark. Typing another question mark displays a list of all commands.

elm command-line options

UNIXspeak

```
elm [-a] [-h] [-f file] [-s subject] -v [recipients]
```

Option or Argument	Function
-f *file*	Reads mail from *file* rather than from your usual mailbox.
-h	Displays help about the elm program.
-s *subject*	Sets subject when sending mail (applies only if you specify a recipient too, for sending mail without first seeing the message index).
-v	Reports elm's version number.
recipients	Sets the name (or names) of recipient (or recipients) when you're sending mail. This option is for sending mail without first seeing the message index.

Part VI

The Network

This part of the book tells you how to use remote computers (computers other than the one you usually use) and transfer files to or from other computers.

Most UNIX systems have built-in networking. Your computer is probably attached to many others and may even be attached to the global Internet. (Some UNIX systems still use only the old uucp dial-up network, which is not discussed here.)

For info about uucp, see the section "A Really Gross Old Network" in Chapter 28 of *UNIX For Dummies*.

Logging In to a Remote Computer By Using telnet

telnet is used to attach to another computer so that you can give it commands and possibly access its files. telnet works on all sorts of networked computers, but only ones that run UNIX.

UNIXspeak

telnet [*computername*]

Option or Argument	Function
host	Specifies the computer you want to use

Steps

1. To log in to another computer, type telnet and the name of the computer, like this:

   telnet computername

2. The telnet program connects. In its greeting message, it tells you its "escape" character, usually Ctrl-]. Make a note of it — you may need it later. Now everything you type is sent to the remote computer, and its responses are returned to your screen.

3. The other computer usually asks you to log in. Log in as though you had just dialed directly into the other computer.

4. Use the remote computer by giving whatever commands make it jump.

5. To leave telnet, log out of the other computer, usually by using the logout or exit commands.

More stuff

If the other computer doesn't let you log out, try this procedure:

1. Type the "escape" character reported by telnet when it started.

2. If telnet doesn't say something like telnet> in a second or two, press Enter to force it to do so.

3. Type **quit** and press Enter to make telnet exit.

See the section "Logging In and Out" in Chapter 20 of *UNIX For Dummies*.

Logging In to a Remote Computer By Using rlogin

rlogin is used to attach to another UNIX computer so that you can give it commands and possibly access its files. rlogin is easier to use than telnet.

UNIXspeak

rlogin [-l username] *computername*

Option or Argument	Function
username	Specifies your username on the other computer. If you use the same name on the remote computer as on the computer you are currently using, skip this part.

Option or Argument	Function
computername	Specifies the computer you want to use. The computer must support `rlogin` (most non-UNIX systems don't).

Steps

1. To log in to another computer, type `rlogin` and the name of the computer, like this:

   `rlogin computername`

2. After `rlogin` connects, everything you type is sent to the remote computer, and its responses are returned to your screen. You are usually logged in automatically.

3. To log out, use the `logout` or `exit` commands as usual.

More stuff

If you have trouble escaping from `rlogin`, press Enter, type

`~.`

and then press Enter again. This step should tell `rlogin` to bug off.

If your username on the other computer is different from the local one, type it on the command line by using the `-l` option, like this:

`rlogin shamu -l king`

If you use `rlogin` to access a computer that doesn't have your username in its files, it may ask you to enter a username and password.

See the section "The Lazy Man's Remote Login" in Chapter 20 of *UNIX For Dummies*.

Running One Command at a Time By Using rsh

`rsh` is used to run one program on another computer. This command can be useful for looking at remote directories or using a remote printer.

UNIXspeak

rsh [-l *username*] *computername command*

Option or Argument	Function
username	Specifies your username on the other computer. If you use the same name on the remote computer as on the computer you are currently using, skip this part.
computername	Specifies the computer you want to use. The computer must run UNIX.
command	Specifies the command to run on the remote computer.

More stuff

To run the who command on a computer named shamu, for example, you type

    rsh shamu who

If you have a different username on that computer, use the -l option to include it, like this:

    rsh *computername* -l *yourusername command*

The rsh command does not work with interactive, screen-oriented programs, such as vi or emacs. If you want to use one of them, use rlogin instead.

You can use pipes to pass data from local programs to remote programs by using rsh. To print a local file on a remote computer, for example, type this line:

    pr mylocalfile | rsh shamu lpr

See the section "One Command at a Time" in Chapter 20 of *UNIX For Dummies*.

Checking Up on Other People

Used to check the status of users and remote computers on your network.

UNIXspeak

finger [-s] [*username*][@*computername*]

Option or Argument	Function
-s	Specifies the short form of the display, with less information about the users
usernames	Specifies the user (or users) you want to know about
computername	Specifies the name of the computer on which to check

Steps

To find out about all logged in users on your machine, type

```
finger
```

To find out about a particular user on your machine, whether or not she's logged in, type

```
finger username
```

To find out about all logged-in users on another machine, type

```
finger @computername
```

To find out about a particular user on another machine, type

```
finger username@computername
```

 See the sections "Finding Out Who's on Your Computer" and "Finding Out Who's on Other Computers" in Chapter 17 of *UNIX For Dummies*.

Finding Out Which Files Are on Your Own Computer

Systems called *NFS* (Network File System) and *RFS* (Remote File System) enable you to use files on other computers as though they were on your computer. *Remote files* (files stored on another computer but available to you) generally act almost exactly like the ones on your own computer, just a little slower.

Of the files you have access to, it is not obvious which are stored on your own computer and which are on remote computers. To find out, use the mount command to run a program that is stored in the /etc directory. Knowing where your files are stored can be useful if your files seem to disappear — the remote computer where they live may have crashed.

UNIX'speak

/etc/mount

Steps

1. Type

   /etc/mount

2. The mount command displays a list of the file systems you can use, like this:

   /dev/sd0h on /var type 4.2 (rw)
   shamu:/mnt on /mnt type nfs (rw,bg)
   shamu:/usr/local on /usr/local type nfs (rw,bg)

   If the line begins with /dev, it is on your own computer. If it begin with the name of a computer on your network (such as shamu), it is stored on that computer. In this case, /var is a local disk and /mnt and /usr/local are on machine shamu. The (rw) means that a disk is "read-write" — you can create and change files there if permissions permit.

See the section "My Files Are Where?" in Chapter 19 of *UNIX For Dummies*.

Copying Files with rcp

rcp is used to copy files from one UNIX system to another. The rcp command works very much like the regular cp command.

UNIX'speak

rcp [-p] [-r] [*username@*]*filenames* *newfilename*

Option or Argument	Function
username	Specifies your username on the remote computer, if it is different from the name you use on your usual computer.
-p	Doesn't change the modification time or mode of the files when you are copying them.

Option or Argument	Function
-r	If the *filenames* and *newfilenames* are both directory names rather than filenames, copies all the files and subdirectories in the directory.
filenames	Specifies the files to copy. This argument can be a filename (to copy one file), a filename specification that uses wildcards (to copy a bunch of files), or a directory name (to copy all the files in the directory as well as in its subdirectories).
newfilename	Specifies the names to give to the copied files. This argument can be a filename (when you're copying one file) or a directory name.

Steps

To copy a file from another system to yours, type

```
rcp computername:filename newfilename
```

To copy a file named hound.dog from a system named shamu, for example, and call the new copy whale.dog, type

```
rcp shamu:hound.dog whale.dog
```

To copy a file from your system to another system, type

```
rcp filename computername:newfilename
```

More stuff

If you want to copy files on the remote system that belong to another user, use ~name to say from whose directory to get them. Type

```
rcp computername:~username/filename newfilename
```

If you have a different username on the remote system, put your name and an @ before the computer name. For example:

```
rcp king@shamu:somefile shamufile
```

rcp can copy entire directories by using the -r switch. For example, this command copies all the files in the projectdir directory, including its subdirectories, and stores the copies in the shamudir directory:

```
rcp -r shamu:projectdir shamudir
```

TIP

`rcp` is extremely closed-mouthed. If nothing goes wrong, it doesn't say anything.

REFERENCE

See the section "Blatting Files Across the Network" in Chapter 20 of *UNIX For Dummies*.

Copying Files with `ftp`

`ftp` is used to copy files to and from other computers on the network.

UNIX'speak

> `ftp` [-v] *computername*

Option or Argument	Function
-v	Displays lots of messages to tell you what it's doing
computername	Specifies the computer with which you want to exchange files

Steps

1. Type `ftp` and the name of the computer to copy to or from. For example, type

   `ftp shamu`

2. It tells you when you are connected, with a message like this:

   `Connected to iecc.com.`

   `220 iecc FTP server (Version 4.1 8/1/91) ready.`

3. When it asks, enter your login name and password.

4. It tells you when you are logged in, with a message and prompt like this:

   `230 User elvis logged in.`

   `ftp>`

5. Now you can give `ftp` commands to copy files. But first, if you're going to transfer nontext files, such as word processing documents, compressed files, runnable programs, or other data files, tell the system to use "binary mode" with the `binary` command. Type

   `binary`

6. To see which files are available, use the dir (directory) command. Type

   ```
   dir
   ```

   You see a listing like this:

   ```
   200 PORT command successful.
   150 Opening ASCII mode data connection for .
   total 122
   -rw-rw-r-- 1 elvis staff 496846 Nov 11 21:23 concerts
   -rw-rw-r-- 1 elvis staff 1507 Nov 11 21:27 records
   226 Transfer complete.
   408 bytes received in 0.47 seconds (0.84 Kbytes/s)
   ```

7. To change to a different directory, use the cd command. Type

   ```
   cd directoryname
   ```

8. To retrieve a file from the remote computer, use the get command. Type

   ```
   get remotefile localfile
   ```

   remotefile is the name the file has on the other computer. *localfile* is the name you want to give the new copy on your computer. (You can omit the local filename if it's the same as the remote filename.)

9. To transmit a file to the remote computer, use the put command. Type

   ```
   put localfile remotefile
   ```

   localfile is the name the file has on your computer. *remotefile* is the name you want to give the new copy on the other computer. (You can omit the remote filename if it's the same as the local filename. put works only if the remote system permissions allow you to store files there.)

10. When you finish copying files, type **quit** to leave ftp.

More stuff

To retrieve many files from the remote system, use mget with a wildcard. To retrieve all the files in the current working directory, for example, type

```
mget *
```

For each remote file that matches the name you give (in this case, all of them because * matches any filename), ftp asks you whether you want to copy the file. Type y if you do; n if you don't.

If you don't have an account on the other computer, try using the login name `anonymous` and use your full electronic-mail address as the password. This technique is called an *anonymous* `ftp`.

See the section "The he-man's file-transfer program" in Chapter 20 of *UNIX For Dummies*.

Index

•F•

•T•

•U•

IDG BOOKS WORLDWIDE REGISTRATION CARD

RETURN THIS REGISTRATION CARD FOR FREE CATALOG

Title of this book: UNIX For Dummies Quick Reference

My overall rating of this book: ❏ Very good [1] ❏ Good [2] ❏ Satisfactory [3] ❏ Fair [4] ❏ Poor [5]

How I first heard about this book:

❏ Found in bookstore; name: [6] _____ ❏ Book review: [7] _____

❏ Advertisement: [8] _____ ❏ Catalog: [9] _____

❏ Word of mouth; heard about book from friend, co-worker, etc.: [10] ❏ Other: [11] _____

What I liked most about this book:

_____

_____

What I would change, add, delete, etc., in future editions of this book:

_____

_____

Other comments:

_____

Number of computer books I purchase in a year: ❏ 1 [12] ❏ 2-5 [13] ❏ 6-10 [14] ❏ More than 10 [15]

I would characterize my computer skills as: ❏ Beginner [16] ❏ Intermediate [17] ❏ Advanced [18] ❏ Professional [19]

I use ❏ DOS [20] ❏ Windows [21] ❏ OS/2 [22] ❏ Unix [23] ❏ Macintosh [24] ❏ Other: [25] _____
(please specify)

I would be interested in new books on the following subjects:
(please check all that apply, and use the spaces provided to identify specific software)

❏ Word processing: [26] _____ ❏ Spreadsheets: [27] _____

❏ Data bases: [28] _____ ❏ Desktop publishing: [29] _____

❏ File Utilities: [30] _____ ❏ Money management: [31] _____

❏ Networking: [32] _____ ❏ Programming languages: [33] _____

❏ Other: [34] _____

I use a PC at (please check all that apply): ❏ home [35] ❏ work [36] ❏ school [37] ❏ other: [38] _____

The disks I prefer to use are ❏ 5.25 [39] ❏ 3.5 [40] ❏ other: [41] _____

I have a CD ROM: ❏ yes [42] ❏ no [43]

I plan to buy or upgrade computer hardware this year: ❏ yes [44] ❏ no [45]

I plan to buy or upgrade computer software this year: ❏ yes [46] ❏ no [47]

Name: _____ Business title: [48] _____

Type of Business: [49] _____

Address (❏ home [50] ❏ work [51]/Company name: _____)

Street/Suite# _____

City [52]/State [53]/Zipcode [54]: _____ Country [55] _____

❏ I liked this book!
You may quote me by name in future IDG Books Worldwide promotional materials.

My daytime phone number is _____

IDG BOOKS

THE WORLD OF COMPUTER KNOWLEDGE

☐ YES!

Please keep me informed about IDG's World of Computer Knowledge. Send me the latest IDG Books catalog.